FOCUS ON
Presentations

W9-BMM-562

FOCUS ON *Presentations*

Peter Lovrick
George Brown College

THOMSON

NELSON

Australia   Canada   Mexico   Singapore   Spain   United Kingdom   United States

Focus on Presentations

by Peter Lovrick

Associate Vice President, Editorial Director:
Evelyn Veitch

Executive Editor:
Rod Banister

Senior Executive Marketing Manager:
Don Thompson

Senior Developmental Editor:
Joanne Sutherland

Permissions Coordinator:
Kristiina Bowering

Senior Production Editor:
Natalia Denesiuk

Copy Editor & Proofreader:
Joan Rawlin

Production Coordinator:
Ferial Suleman

Design Director:
Ken Phipps

Interior Design:
Tammy Gay

Cover Design:
Katherine Strain

Cover Image:
© Corel

Compositor:
Carol Magee

Printer:
Transcontinental

COPYRIGHT © 2006 by Nelson, a division of Thomson Canada Limited.

Printed and bound in Canada
1 2 3 4 08 07 06 05

For more information contact Nelson, 1120 Birchmount Road, Toronto, Ontario, M1K 5G4. Or you can visit our Internet site at http://www.nelson.com

ALL RIGHTS RESERVED. No part of this work covered by the copyright herein may be reproduced, transcribed, or used in any form or by any means—graphic, electronic, or mechanical, including photocopying, recording, taping, Web distribution, or information storage and retrieval systems—without the written permission of the publisher.

For permission to use material from this text or product, submit a request online at www.thomsonrights.com

Every effort has been made to trace ownership of all copyrighted material and to secure permission from copyright holders. In the event of any question arising as to the use of any material, we will be pleased to make the necessary corrections in future printings.

Library and Archives Canada Cataloguing in Publication Data

Main entry under title:

Lovrick, Peter, 1953–

    Focus on presentations / Peter Lovrick.

ISBN 0-17-641539-4

    1. Public speaking. 2. Business presentations. 3. Verbal ability.
I. Title.

HF5718.22.L69 2005   808.5'1
C2005-901103-3

Table of Contents

Preface

This book gives you two goals to work toward. The first is to develop your presentation skills so that you become the best presenter you can possibly be. The second is to help your classmates develop their skills so that they can be the best presenters they can possibly be. To reach these goals, you will work through a series of tasks that ask you to discover for yourself what techniques and components will work for you. The tasks ask you to work with other people, investigate different resources, and analyze your own experience. As you help other people hone their presentation skills, you will develop an instinct for giving presentations on your own. As others help you, they will also learn valuable lessons.

The approach in *Focus on Presentations* is to ask you to take charge of your own learning. That means you need to take initiative to find out rather than wait to be told. It also means that you share what you discover. Finally, you need to be a creative problem solver. Apply that problem solving to the issues around working with others for common goals and to finding the information you need to successfully complete the assignments.

Here's what to expect.

You will work in small groups.

The cooperative learning approach in this book asks you to work with other people and pool your knowledge. It isn't necessary to agree with everything you hear. It is necessary, though, to be a good listener, to give everyone a chance to contribute, and to critically evaluate how helpful the discussion is to your own presentations. Each unit presents you with a series of problems or tasks designed for four people, but you can still carry them out with a different number. That's where your problem solving comes in. You have many options. If you have fewer than four people, you might decide to split up the work of person four, or visit another group for the missing piece. If you have more than four, you can have two people work on one task, or work out a rotation so that a different person is an observer each time. Your group is in charge of how you manage the issues and challenges. Be creative.

You will keep a group portfolio.

Your group will keep a common portfolio. Your instructor will give it to your group at the beginning of class and collect it at the end. It is your communication tool with the instructor. Use it to submit your assignments, outlines, and forms. Your instructor will use it to give you feedback, evaluations, announcements, and other material.

You will present individual work.

You will meet in groups, but the presentations you give are you own. Keep in mind that as you prepare and work toward those presentations, the help and advice of other people will give you the tools you need to refine your work so that you can give highly effective and successful presentations.

You will uncover the information you need as you need it.

This book does not simply supply information that the author has decided you should have. Instead, your group will look at the different tasks, decide what it needs, and go get it. Your answers may be very different from other groups working on the same projects. Far from anything being wrong with that, it will be a wonderful opportunity to see different perspectives in action. You have several resources to work with to accomplish the tasks set out for you.

The Internet

The Internet offers a wide variety of Web sites that you can consult for this book. You will find helpful addresses at different points in the book, but look beyond these sites to find whatever information you need to complete the speaking tasks. Be creative in your search and use alternative search terms. "Public speaking," "presentations," "speeches," and "speech making" are just some of the terms that will take you to sites offering advice and tips that you can bring to your group discussions. Look at the educational sites first. You can identify them by the extensions .ca or .edu.

Libraries

Several excellent texts on public speaking are on the market. Two wonderful books are Judith Rolls' *Public Speaking Made Easy* and Clella Jaffe's *Public Speaking*. Check them out and see what else is on the shelves of your public or college library. Some of the tasks ahead will ask you to do some research into specific components of public speaking. Look at the literature available and bring the results to your group.

Interviews with People Who Give Presentations

Think about the people you know who give presentations. Teachers come to mind first, but many professions today require presentations from making sales pitches to training new hires. Talk to some of these people to get the information you need to develop your own skills.

Your Instructor

Your instructor has expertise in presentation skills. Consult your instructor as a special resource. Test out ideas, ask questions, and invite comments on the ideas your group develops.

Your Own Experience

Many of the tasks in this book ask you to think about your own experience either as a presenter or as a listener. Rely on what your experience shows you works or doesn't work. Analyze that experience in the tasks ahead and share what you learn from that analysis with your group members.

You will reflect on all the work you do.

An essential part of this approach is to reflect on your work after a series of tasks or presentations is complete. The book will give you different tools to do just that. You will assess the work of your group partners and think critically about what you have done. In this way, you will identify the characteristics and techniques of great presentations.

About the Author

Peter Lovrick has been a professor at George Brown College since 1987. He teaches presentation skills, technical/business writing, report and thesis writing, and communications for internationally trained professionals. His CV includes teaching philosophical writing, philosophical reading, and homiletics. He has also taught History of Chinese Performing Arts at the University of Toronto for over 10 years and Writing, Modern Drama, and Shakespeare at Soochow University in Taiwan.

Peter has also authored *Chinese Opera: Images and Stories* (1997), published by the University of British Columbia Press, which was shortlisted for the 1997 Kiriyama Book Prize.

He is married to Theresa and has three beautiful children: Adrian, Katrina, and Anthony. Ordained as a Permanent Deacon for the Archdiocese of Toronto, Peter is also currently working on a doctorate.

Acknowledgements

I gratefully acknowledge the inspiration of Dr. Idahlynn Karre whose presentations on cooperative learning opened up an entirely new pedagogy for me. Kay Oxford and Joyce Kraay, professors at George Brown College, have been supportive and encouraging. I am glad to count them not just as colleagues, but as friends. Finally, Joanne Sutherland of Thomson Nelson publishing gave invaluable help for the format and final draft of this book. Her suggestions were always right on the mark.

Thanks also go to the following reviewers whose thoughtful comments helped shape *Focus on Presentations*.

Dave Banninga, Niagara College

Brent Cotton, Georgian College

Jill Hynes, Georgian College

Linda Large, Canadore College

Andrea Lovering, Georgian College

David Patient, Simon Fraser University

Mark Rust, Sheridan College

Jill Tomasson Goodwin, University of Waterloo

Part 1

Preparation

Part 1 introduces you to the work-group concept upon which this book is based. It also gives you the opportunity to gain knowledge and skills that are fundamental to giving an effective presentation. In Unit 2, you will learn how to deal with presentation anxiety. As you work through that unit, you will identify specific strategies for managing any nervousness you might have. Good listening and critiquing skills are also essential if you are going to give effective help to others in the class. Units 3 and 4 will help you reflect on your skills and identify specific ways to improve them. Finally, a vital part of your preparation for any presentation is to know your audience. Unit 5 will present a method that you can use to target your talks to specific groups of people.

UNIT 1

Getting the Most Out of This Book

Here's what you'll work on in this unit.

- Setting individual objectives
- Writing a goal statement
- Creating a work group
- Interviewing a team member
- Making your first presentation
- Determining the occasions for presentations in your field
- Identifying the types of presentations
- Validating a successful presentation

Many people find presentations a challenge. Some feel self-conscious or embarrassed when speaking in front of a group. Others feel right at home. Those who don't feel that way often wish they had more self-assurance. Actually, there is no great secret to delivering effective presentations. It really comes down to experience. Through experience, you overcome excessive nervousness. Through experience, you also discover what works and what doesn't work. One of the most helpful things along the way is also learning from the experience of others. Some tips they have discovered will work for you while others just won't fit your own unique style.

Focus on Presentations is organized to help you get the most of out speaking experiences. Whether your class is large or small, you will work through the tasks in this book in small groups. The small group approach is designed to give you the benefits of collaborative learning. You will help each other to deliver the best presentations you possibly can. In addition, you will get the different perspectives of team members who are working through their own challenges. That's where learning happens. Improving presentation skills is not a matter of a lot of lectures or extensive reading. It is a matter of doing and reflecting on the doing. That's what you will find in this book.

On Target

The first thing to do before you start a presentations book like this one is establish your goals. When you do that right at the beginning, you ensure that you will be focused on all the benefits that the book's exercises and instruction can bring. In the end, it helps you set the tone for a positive learning experience. Take a few moments and think about it. When you get to the end of this book, you will work on a task that asks you to evaluate whether or not you have reached some or all of the targets you set for yourself.

Setting Your Goals   TASK ONE

Here's what to do. First, write down as many specific objectives as you want in the box entitled Personal Objectives below. Leave the box entitled Additional Objectives (on page 4) blank for now. Here are some questions to help you with this task.

- What specific aspects of giving a presentation would you like to work on?
- What can you already do in a presentation that you would like to be able to do even better?
- What new presentation abilities would you like learn?
- What is it that you would like for yourself, when you have finished this book?
- Imagine yourself giving the final presentation. What skills would you like to be able to demonstrate then?

Hint

Keep your answers very specific and focused on particular skills, so that at the end of the book you will be able to say whether or not you have developed them.

Personal Objectives

Additional Objectives

Now, look over the different individual objectives you wrote in the box. Do some of them connect? Do some specific objectives belong to larger goals? Are there one or two main goals that stand out? Spend a little time reconsidering your points and then write out a general goal statement in full sentences. If you have only one or two sentences, or a full paragraph, that's okay. Think about how you would answer the following question. What would you like to achieve here?

Hint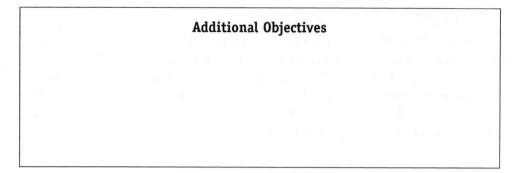

While an objective is a specific skill you would like to develop, a goal is the larger destination to which the objectives point. Think of it this way: why do you want to accomplish the specific objectives? Why is it important to reach each of those targets?

Goal Statement

As you go through the book, you will likely discover other skills that you will want to work on. That's what the Additional Objectives box is for. Just write them in as they come up. Refer back to this page at various times as you move through this book to see how you're doing. Are you making progress? Are you learning and mastering the skills that you set out for yourself?

Getting Started

To move ahead with the projects in this text, you need to get into a work group. The tasks work best if your group is small and has an even number of people. Four works best. If that isn't possible for your group, divide the instructions for each of the tasks as evenly as possible among the group members. Each person needs to take a number that identifies him or her as 1, 2, 3, or 4. The group members will help you accomplish your goal statement and meet your specific objectives and you will help them do the same. That means pooling ideas, contributing to the completion of tasks, critiquing each other's work, and being an audience for each other. The place to start, then, is to get to know each other a little better.

Meeting the Group

Person 1: Facilitate this activity. Read out the directions below.

Person 2: Keep track of the time.

Part One

1. The group manager makes sure everyone in the group has a partner. Each person is designated A or B.
2. A interviews B for 10 minutes. A takes notes to find out whatever B is willing to share about likes, dislikes, background, personality, hopes, goals, or anything that comes to mind. B also reads out the goal statement from Task One.
3. B interviews A for 10 minutes and takes notes. A, too, reads out the goal statement from Task One and answers questions on whatever he or she is willing to share.

Part Two

Everyone takes five minutes to organize the notes from the interview and prepare a short presentation that introduces the person interviewed to the team. Starting with person 1, everyone gives the introductory presentation.

Step Up and Present

Hint

Rearrange the information from the interview. Rather than reciting questions and answers in the order asked, put all the information together to create a total picture of a person. Finally, work out a beginning, middle, and end.

The introduction of your partner to a small group was your first presentation in this book. That task actually summarized what any presentation requires you to do. You had to

- keep a specific purpose in mind,
- do some research,
- organize the information,
- select what you wanted to emphasize or leave out, and
- deliver it to a specific audience.

You likely delivered it in a very casual way because you automatically sized up your audience. What if you were introducing the same person in a boardroom situation, or as the speaker at a conference? Would you have introduced your partner in the same way? What is appropriate in one place just doesn't fit in another. When you present longer and more complex presentations in future exercises, you will continue to work through the same process. The exercises and tasks will ask you to reflect on the decisions you make.

Occasions for Presentations

Look at any job listing in the newspaper or on the Web. Good communications skills are a must-have today. Your first contact with an employer is likely to be the job interview. Many people haven't thought of an interview as a presentation, but it is, in fact, a vital one. When you find that dream job or that perfect place of employment, you will have a great deal riding on how well you perform in the 20 to 30 minutes it takes to be interviewed. That's why one of the presentation situations you work on later in this book is the job interview. Occasions for presentations in the workplace don't stop there, though. There are a great many professional situations in which you can be called upon to speak in front of others.

TASK THREE   Professional Speaking Situations

Part One

Identify some of the occupations in your field. Compile a list of as many situations as you can think of when those occupations might require presentations. How do these presentation situations differ from one another?

Person 3: Facilitate this task. Make sure that everyone has an opportunity to talk, and keep the discussion focused on the topic.

Person 4: Record the results of the discussion in the table provided on page 7 and be prepared to present the results to the entire class when called upon. Leave the columns entitled Category and Validation blank for the time being.

Hint

If everyone in the group is entering the same field, select about four different occupations within the one field. If group members are entering different fields, identify the fields and a particular occupation within each one.

OCCASIONS FOR PROFESSIONAL PRESENTATIONS

Occupation	Presentation	How Does the Presentation Differ From Others?	Category	Validation

Once you get started on compiling a list like the one on page 7, you begin to see just how wide the opportunities for giving presentations really are. Some professionals give sales pitches. Others present various reports. Some are responsible for instructing and training. Yet others have to make a case to an employer or a client. In your own case, the employer may decide to send you to a seminar or a conference and then expect you to present to your colleagues when you get back. You might not like the direction a staff meeting is taking and just have to get up and say something. All of these situations call upon your skills as a presenter. In addition, you can be called upon to make even more presentations in your personal life. You might be asked to speak at a friend's wedding, a family event, clubs, organizations, or community groups.

The range of presentation opportunities is wide, but there are really only a few basic types. Table 1.1 shows one way of categorizing presentations.

TABLE 1.1 TYPES OF PRESENTATIONS

Entertaining	Some presentations are purely for entertainment. The main purpose of the stand-up comic and the storyteller is to provide a good show for their audience.
Informative	Many presentations are put together in order to convey information. The classroom lecture and the news briefing are structured so that the audience understands something it did not understand before.
Instructive	Instructive presentations are closely connected to informative ones. The big difference is that the presenter doesn't want you to just understand something; he or she wants you to be able to do something as well. A swimming instructor doesn't want you to understand swimming only theoretically. The important thing is that you can swim the length of the pool. A health and safety trainer needs to be sure that staff knows how to follow safety procedures.
Persuasive	A great many presentations are persuasive. These are both the most common and the most difficult to get right. All your presentations are important, but these are vital. You want that job. You want that sale. You want to convince others to follow your plan.
Inspirational	Many situations require the inspirational presentation. A sports team needs a pep talk. A company needs to boost morale. A religious group needs encouragement or consolation. Your team in the workplace might need to be hyped up for a special project or pulled together if something goes wrong.

You will discover that your presentations seem to be a combination of several basic categories. Your persuasive presentation contains a great deal of information. Your informative presentation starts off with a joke. Your instructive presentation has a strong persuasive note because you want to be sure that the listeners don't take any dangerous shortcuts. Still, each presentation you give will primarily fit in one category or another.

Person 2:   Manage the group discussion for the following group task.

Go back over your group's list of occasions for professional presentations. Categorize the different presentations you came up with as primarily entertaining, informative, instructive, persuasive, or inspirational. Are there any presentations on your list that don't seem to fit primarily in one of those categories? Do you need to develop an additional category? If so, discuss it, come up with a name, and let the rest of the class know your idea.

Person 1:   Write the name of the category that the group identifies in the Category column on the right.

Validation

Your professional presentations matter. They have to be a success. You really want the client or the employer to buy into your proposal. You really want your point of view to carry the day in the staff meeting. That means that planning a presentation has to be focused on particular results. A driving instructor knows if training was successful only when the students can parallel park. A sales pitch is successful only when the sale is made. A lecturer knows that an informative presentation was successful when the listeners are able to describe and explain the same subject in their own words. Whether you give a formal presentation like the projects later in this book or an informal one like the introductions in Task Two, ask yourself some questions first. Just what is your measure of success? How will you know that you accomplished your basic purpose?

Person 4:   Manage the group discussion for the following group task.

Look through the list of professional presentations one last time. Decide how the presenter would know whether or not the presentation was successful.

Person 3:   Write the method the group decides upon for each of the speaking tasks in the column entitled Validation.

Hint

If you are not sure how a presenter would determine success in a particular situation, leave the validation column blank. Determine the best way to find out the answer and who will bring it to the next class. The group might decide that asking someone in the field is best. It may also decide to consult with an instructor of the vocational subject.

You have now looked through a number of speaking tasks, decided in which category they fit, and what tool could be used to determine whether or not they accomplished what they set out to do. That's really just the bare minimum. Many presentations can accomplish the goal, but some shine above the rest. These presentations are especially effective because they apply techniques suitable for their own special purposes. The presenter in such cases also has strong delivery skills. These techniques and skills are the focus of each of the following units. In the meantime, it's time to share some of your work with others in a second presentation.

TASK SIX   Feedback

Step Up and Present

Person 2: Take the Occasion for Presentations sheet to another group. Briefly explain the different speaking occasions your group came up with, the categories, and your validation method. Be prepared to take any questions that the other group might have. When you finish, return to your group with any feedback or questions your audience had. The group can then decide if it wants to make revisions to the sheet.

In Summary

Take three minutes to write a summary of what you learned from participating in the tasks of Unit 1.

_____

_____

_____

_____

_____

_____

_____

_____

_____

_____

_____

_____

_____

_____

UNIT 2

Presentation Anxiety

Here's what you'll work on in this unit.

- Determining your presentation comfort level
- Creating a table of common concerns when giving presentations
- Identifying your own anxiety factors
- Discovering techniques for overcoming anxiety
- Researching and developing a guide for the nervous speaker
- Preparing a presentation

Your Comfort Level

How do you feel about presenting in front of people? Some people are very comfortable with the idea. They look forward to opportunities to stand up and speak to a group. Others are not so sure. They would much rather work on a long written assignment than deliver a short oral one. Some become tense, tongue-tied, and even panicky. Where do you fit? Think about the questions below. They ask you to size up how you feel when asked to give a presentation in front of a group people. You will probably feel differently depending on who those people are or just how many of them are in your audience. For the purpose of this exercise, assume that you have been asked to speak to a group of about 50 of your peers. After you have looked over the questions, decide where you would place yourself on the comfort scale and circle the number that you judge best reflects where you are now.

Placing Yourself on the Comfort Scale · TASK ONE

Tell your group members where you are on the comfort scale. Explain why you gave yourself the number you did. Tell the group a particular instance or example when you gave a presentation and how you felt at the time.

TABLE 2.1 PRESENTATION SKILLS COMFORT SCALE

1	2	3	4	5
Does the idea of making a presentation really scare you? Would you rather do just about anything else?	Are you so nervous that you might freeze up and forget everything? Are you worried that the audience will not like you or that they might even laugh at you? Are you so nervous that your anxiety shows in your voice, face, or body movement? Are you concerned that you might not do as well as you would like?	Does your heart beat faster? Do you feel butterflies in your stomach?	Does the idea of giving a presentation appeal to you? Do you feel excited when you have the opportunity to give one? Can you visualize yourself giving an effective presentation?	Are you completely relaxed? Does the idea of giving a presentation cause you no anxiety at all?

Person 1: Manage this activity. Keep the group discussion on topic. Give everyone a chance to tell the group where he or she is on the comfort scale. Ask them to explain the answer and share an example.

Person 2: Keep time for this exercise. The total time is 12 minutes (3 minutes per person). Keep the group posted.

Person 3: Keep track of the different numbers in the Group Profile below.

GROUP PROFILE

Comfort Scale Number	Number of People	Comfort Scale
1		Very Anxious
2		Anxious
3		Somewhat Anxious
4		Somewhat Confident
5		Very Confident

Many people share a fear of speaking in public to one degree or another. It is often listed among the top stress factors along with moving and death. For some, the nervousness is a major challenge to overcome; for others it is often debilitating. Just why do so many people feel that way? If you or your group members experience any anxiety over speaking in front of others, consider what it is that really bothers you. Identifying what concerns you is the first step in developing specific techniques for confidence.

Determining Common Concerns   TASK TWO

Create a table of common concerns connected with public speaking anxiety. Determine which ones, if any, you share. Add items to the list that you see are missing.

Person 4: Read the following article to your group.

Person 3: Manage the group as it creates a table from the data in the article that shows the specific fears or concerns and the percentages connected with them. Use the first two columns of the table that follows. Ask your group members which of these concerns affects them. Indicate the responses in the column entitled Your Group.

Person 2: Facilitate a group discussion around what additional items should be added to this list. Write them down as they come up. It is not necessary to have group consensus.

Public-speaking Fears in a Community Sample. Prevalence, Impact on Functioning, and Diagnostic Classification

M. B. Stein, J. R. Walker, and D. R. Forde
Department of Psychiatry, University of Manitoba, Winnipeg

Background
Recent epidemiologic studies have revealed that social phobia is more prevalent than has been previously believed. An unresolved issue is the extent to which public-speaking fears constitute a recognizable form of social phobia in a community sample, and, moreover, to what extent these fears are associated with functional morbidity.

Methods
To examine the prevalence and impact of public-speaking fears and their relationship to social phobia in a community sample, we conducted a randomized telephone survey of 499 residents of Winnipeg, Manitoba, a medium-sized midwestern metropolitan area.

(cont'd)

Results

One third of the respondents reported that they had excessive anxiety when they spoke to a large audience. The onset of fears was early (i.e., 50%, 75%, and 90% by the ages of 13, 17, and 20 years, respectively). Anxious cognitions about public speaking included the following fears: doing or saying something embarrassing (64%), one's mind going blank (74%), being unable to continue talking (63%), saying foolish things or not making sense (59%), and trembling, shaking, or showing other signs of anxiety (80%). In total, 10% (n = 49) of the respondents reported that public-speaking anxiety had resulted in a marked interference with their work (2%), social life (1%), or education (4%), or had caused them marked distress (8%). Twenty-three persons (5%) had public-speaking anxiety in isolation (i.e., without evidence of additional kinds of social fears).

Conclusions

These data support the inclusion of severe forms of public-speaking fears within the social phobia construct, and, furthermore, suggest that public-speaking anxiety may have a detrimental impact on the lives of many individuals in the community.

Source: JAMA & Archives Web site, Archives of General Psychiatry http://archpsyc.ama-assn.org/cgi/content/abstract/53/2/169

SPECIFIC CONCERNS WHEN GIVING A PRESENTATION

Concern	Percentage	Your Group

Overcoming Anxiety

You now have a clear profile of how comfortable your group is with giving presentations and what particular issues are of most concern to the people with whom you are working. The next step is to see what you can do to overcome some of these problems.

Actually, it's good if you have some degree of nervousness. If you're nervous, that means you care about the presentation. You want to do well. Your nervousness gets your heart pumping and gives you that extra bit of energy that can help you give a dynamic talk. The fact is, you need extra energy if you are going to get that volume to fill the room and carry your message across in a strong, effective manner. If you're very relaxed it might be because you're an old pro, but it also might mean that you're treating the presentation too casually. It's better to have that nervous edge. Professional speakers and actors will tell you that no matter how many times they have been in front of people, they still experience butterflies. If you feel those butterflies, too, treat that as a sign that you are going to have an energetic delivery. The idea, then, is to channel the energy from your nerves and make it useful. Nervousness doesn't have to paralyze; it can energize.

How do you channel that energy? How do you reduce a bad case of nerves? Here are a few tips to get you started on your next group exercise.

Prepare

One of the surest ways to reduce anxiety is to prepare thoroughly. A well-prepared presentation gives you confidence. You know what you are talking about. You have got all the bases covered. In later units, you will work on projects that require you to research your topic and your audience. That research and a strong outline can go a long way to making you feel good about giving a presentation.

Rehearse

Certain presentation situations require you to speak impromptu, that means without any rehearsal. Many others, however, give you the time to practise first. Take advantage of that time and try out your presentation, first to yourself and then to someone close to you. When you have gone through it once or twice, you know that you can do it. What's more, the more you rehearse those presentations, the more you are actually building up skills that will help you do effective impromptu presentations later.

Use Visuals

Consider working with visuals in your presentation. A visual can be an object you hold or point to, a projection or just about anything that you bring in to illustrate your points. Visuals can help reduce your tension because they give you something to work with. For a moment you don't need to look at the audience, and for a moment you know that the audience is not looking at you. You have something to point to and direct your energy to. It can even help you remember your next points. You will work on how to put visuals into a talk later in this book.

Develop a list of techniques in addition to the three listed above that can help a presenter reduce anxiety. The following parts will guide you through this task. Pool the results and discuss them in your group to create a guide for the nervous speaker. The guide's title is How to Give a Confident Presentation.

Part One

Everyone does independent research, compiles a list of at least five techniques for reducing nervousness, and brings that list to a group discussion in the next session.

Here are some resources that group members can check out.

1. Explore different resources on the Net for dealing with nervousness in public speaking.

Hint

Start with recognized sites from organizations that specialize in training for public speaking. Two examples are http://www.toastmasters.org/tips.asp and http://www.public-speaking.org/public-speaking-stagefright-article.htm

2. Interview someone who regularly gives presentations. You could find an instructor, a cleric, or a salesperson. What methods does the speaker use to give a confident presentation? What does the speaker consider to be the most important aspect of public speaking?
3. See what public speaking texts are available in your library. Do these have any practical tips that your group members would find useful?

Hint

Excellent text sources are Judith Rolls' *Public Speaking Made Easy* and Clella Jaffe's *Public Speaking*.

Part Two

Person 1: Manage the group discussion so that it stays on topic. Give everyone an equal opportunity to share what was learned. After the last person reports, lead the group in compiling the different techniques into one list.

Person 2: Record the different techniques for the group as they are reported. Group the same kinds of techniques together. After the final discussion, enter the techniques into the table on pages 17 and 18.

HOW TO GIVE A CONFIDENT PRESENTATION

Method	Effect
Prepare	➤ Gives solid content and the assurance that you know your subject
Rehearse	➤ Develops comfort with the presentation and allows you to adjust any trouble spots ahead of time
Use Visuals	➤ Gives you something physical to work with and illustrates your presentation

Method	Effect

Person 3: Take your guide and visit two other groups. Explain to them how these techniques can help.

Person 4: After two visitors have presented to your group, add any new techniques that your group wants to put on the list.

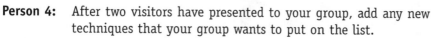

Your group now has a list of techniques to help manage nervousness and build confidence. Use them in later units as you get ready to deliver a variety of presentations. Try them out and discover which ones work best for you. Cross out those that don't seem to help you, and add any new ones that you pick up along the way.

In Summary

Take three minutes to write a summary of what you learned from participating in the tasks of Unit 2.

UNIT 3

Effective Listening Skills

Here's what you'll work on in this unit.

- Examining research on listening
- Determining the difference between listening and hearing
- Analyzing listening case studies
- Identifying different types of noise
- Analyzing a personal listening situation
- Determining effective listening strategies
- Organizing a group presentation

You will give several presentations as you work through this book. Each one of them will require you to prepare, plan, rehearse, deliver, and reflect, but you have another important responsibility, too. That responsibility is to listen. You will have to listen both as a presenter and as a member of the audience. As a speaker, you will need to listen to your audience in many ways. Developing your sensitivity to the kinds of messages your audience sends you will help you to hone your presentation skills. As a member of the audience, you will need to listen carefully to the speaker. The activities in this book will frequently ask you to provide useful feedback so that presenters know what they are doing well and what they need to polish. That feedback depends on how attentive you are to the presentation. Other presentation situations may not require you to give any kind of formal feedback, but effective listening skills are still essential for you to get the most out of each occasion.

The problem is that while many people spend time improving the way they speak, not as many spend time improving the way they listen. Listening, however, is a critical component of any presentation. The listener has a vital role to play in the success of any communication. That is why it is important to reflect on exactly what listening is. Just as you have identified elements for presenting better, determining tips for listening better will make you a better communicator all around.

We often use different words interchangeably for the same concept. Two words that are frequently used are "hearing" and "listening." What do they really mean? Is it possible to hear, but not to listen? In this task, you and your group will to explore what listening is all about.

Part One

Person 2: Read out the following article to your group. Ask the group to close their books and listen rather than read along with you.

Listening Factoids

Listening is important because ...
- Since the rise of the radio and the development of television, the spoken word has regained much of its lost stature (Bryant).
- Being listened to means we are taken seriously, our ideas and feelings are known, and, ultimately, what we have to say matters (Nichols).
- Generous listening enhances our own well-being and is the natural perspective of psychology, in which all human behavior is seen as motivated by the agendas of the self (Nichols).
- We learn our culture largely through listening; we learn to think by listening; we learn to love by listening; we learn about ourselves by listening (Robinson).
- Being listened to spells the difference between feeling accepted and feeling isolated (Nichols).
- In our society, listening is essential to the development and survival of the individual (Robinson).
- Most people will not really listen or pay attention to your point of view until they become convinced you have heard and appreciate theirs (Nichols).

Some interesting statistics ...
- How much of what we know that we have learned by listening? 85% (Shorpe)
- Amount of the time we are distracted, preoccupied, or forgetful? 75% (Hunsaker)
- How much we usually recall immediately after we listen to someone talk? 50% (Robinson)
- Amount of time we spend listening? 45% (Robinson)
- How much we remember of what we hear? 20% (Shorpe)
- Amount of us who have had formal educational experience with listening? less than 2% (Gregg)

And other numbers ...
- We listen at 125–250 words per minute, but think at 1000–3000 words per minute (HighGain, Inc.).
- Number of business studies that indicate that listening is a top skill needed for success in business? more than 35 (HighGain, Inc.)

Source: International Listening Association Web site http://www.listen.org/pages/factoids.html

Person 4: Facilitate this exercise. Ask each person in the group to state one specific fact that they heard during the reading of the article without consulting their text. Verify the information by checking the article as you go.

Person 3: Give one of the following quotes from the article to each person in the group. Ask that person to refer to it in the text and spend a few minutes thinking about the implications of the fact and organizing a two-minute presentation to the group.

1. We listen at 125–250 words per minute, but think at 1000–3000 words per minute (HighGain, Inc.). Amount of the time we are distracted, pre-occupied, or forgetful? 75% (Hunsaker)

2. Amount of time we spend listening? 45% (Robinson). How much we remember of what we hear? 20% (Shorpe)

3. Being listened to means we are taken seriously, our ideas and feelings are known, and, ultimately, what we have to say matters (Nichols). Most people will not really listen or pay attention to your point of view until they become convinced you have heard and appreciate theirs (Nichols).

4. How much of what we know that we have learned by listening? 85% (Shorpe). Amount of us who have had formal educational experience with listening? less than 2% (Gregg)

Hint

Think about what the quote means in terms of the presentations you have given and will give both in this and in other settings. What does this information suggest about the kinds of challenges public speakers face? What kinds of solutions would fit these challenges?

Everyone gives a presentation to the group beginning with person 1.

Step Up and Present

Part Two

Person 1: Facilitate a discussion that defines the difference between hearing and listening. Arrive at a group consensus for the box below.

HEARING IS

_____

_____

_____

_____

LISTENING IS

_____

▷

Listening to the Speaker

Identify the listening challenges in the following situations.

Case One

You are in a classroom listening to a lecture in an elective subject. The course is not part of your field, but graduation requirements include a number of breadth courses. The lights have been dimmed because the professor has put the presentation on PowerPoint. It is hot, so the door has been propped open. Every few moments, students walk by chatting about different subjects. Two students in the back are clearly not interested and are whispering.

CHALLENGES INCLUDE

_____

Case Two

You are at a hall for a special talk at a convention. You have been instructed to write a summary of the presentation. Several people are switching seats, going back to the book displays, or asking to squeeze past you for a seat further in. The speaker is dealing with a complex subject involving specialized terminology. His voice echoes and there is occasional feedback in the sound system.

CHALLENGES INCLUDE

_____

Case Three

Yesterday, you received some disturbing medical news about a family member. Today, you are in a group meeting for a project. The group leader is presenting the specifications of the project and outlining a proposed method to accomplish the task. The group leader talks mostly to the others because she has never really liked you from the start.

CHALLENGES INCLUDE

_____

_____

_____

_____

Noise

Different kinds of noise can interfere with listening. In some cases, the noise is external. Cars outside the window, a loud air-conditioning system, or even a rainstorm can be distracting enough to pull your attention away. Even if the distraction lasts just a moment or two, the damage is done. You may find that you have missed a key point or an important link. Consequently, you find it hard to follow now. That only encourages you to give in to more distractions. In other cases, the noise is internal. You may have plans or problems that are claiming your attention. The presentation might be wonderful, but your internal noise is so loud or attractive that you find yourself listening to that first. Internal noise can also develop when you engage in an internal dialogue with the speaker. Formulating objections, refusing to hear out an argument, or deciding to find fault can filter out some useful information. Finally, noise can also come from the presenter. If the presenter has an annoying habit, or in some way attracts attention to him or herself through dress or behaviour, you can easily find yourself focusing on these externals. You might miss the message of the presentation entirely, or if you get it, your acceptance of it can easily be coloured by how you reacted to the presenter.

Hint

You might not be able to do much about external or presenter noise, but you can do something about internal noise.

Choose a recent listening situation. It might be the last class you attended, a public talk you heard, or a briefing at work. Analyze that situation using the chart below.

Listening Situation		
Motivation to Be There		
External Noise	**Internal Noise**	**Presenter Noise**
Effect on My Listening	**Effect on My Listening**	**Effect on My Listening**
How I Would Rate My Enjoyment of the Presentation?		
If I Attended the Same Presentation Again, What Could I Do to Make It a Better Listening Experience?		

Taking Charge

No one can guarantee that every presentation you go to will be high-powered, engaging, and polished. In fact, you can expect that many presentations will be uninspired and poorly delivered. The problem is that you will likely be expected to go to these presentations anyway. Your professional life, certainly your academic life, will depend on it. If the presentation isn't up to what it should be, your listening skills can make an enormous difference. Here are a couple of things to keep in mind.

- A positive attitude leads to effective listening. Decide that you are going to take away something useful from the presentation, then spend the time looking and listening for it.
- Engaging yourself is another important aspect of good listening skills. You can engage yourself by taking notes, formulating questions to ask later, or asking yourself a question about the subject at the beginning to help guide your listening throughout.

Effective listening skills can be learned and refined. You will have a toolkit of techniques for doing just that after you finish this task.

Part One

Each person in the group works on a set of strategies to improve his or her own listening skills. Resources for this task include Internet sources on listening skills, public-speaking texts, and personal reflection. Bring the list to the group for the next session.

Hint

The group can decide to divide the research among the members according to resource type. One person could focus on Web sites, another on texts, the third on consulting instructors or other experts, and the fourth on periodicals.

Part Two

Person 1: Facilitate this task. Be sure each person has an opportunity to explain the techniques that he or she has found.

Person 2: Enter the different techniques, as they come up, in the table that follows. If any of the techniques repeat, check with the group to see if there is anything different about it that should still be recorded.

Person 3: Keep time. You will be told the amount of time to dedicate to this task. Keep the group aware of how much time it has left.

TECHNIQUES TO IMPROVE LISTENING SKILLS

Technique	Why It Works

Part Three

Person 1: Ask the group to select what it thinks are the top three skills on the list. Organize a five-minute presentation to the entire class entitled "How to Listen Well." Person 1 will deliver an introduction and conclusion. Each of the other group members will present one listening skill, explain why it works, and give an example of how it can be employed.

Your group presents together to all the other groups in the room. Listen carefully to the other groups and add any new techniques to your group's list.

Step Up and Present

In Summary

Take three minutes to write a summary of what you learned from participating in the tasks of Unit 3.

UNIT 4

Criticism: Giving and Taking

Here's what you'll work on in this unit.

- Assessing your knowledge of and response to criticism
- Developing a group policy for criticism
- Analyzing case studies
- Identifying four essential principles of criticism
- Determining the difference between giving feedback and criticism
- Identifying specific techniques for effective criticism
- Developing a short presentation on how to give criticism
- Identifying essential elements of taking criticism

By now you have discovered that you and your team members are your own best teachers. What you have already seen and heard in presentations are all guides to what you can do in yours. The presentations that you will work on, especially the longer ones coming up in later units, are not the ends but the means to reflection and analysis. It is by reflecting on and analyzing the presentations of others and your own that you will discover what works and what doesn't work for you. In that way, your toolkit of skills, your comfort level, and, above all, your instincts for what to do in a presentation will grow dramatically.

But just as listening needs technique, so does criticism. Whether you are criticizing others or your own work, you need to employ a method that will make your analysis useful. Your goal as a critic is to be a teacher and that takes teacher training.

What Criticism Is All About

The first step in your training is to define what criticism is all about. What do you think of when you here the words "criticism" or "critic"? What does it mean to you? Take the following quiz and see what you find out. Check all statements that apply.

THE CRITICISM QUIZ

1. When I hear that someone is coming to criticize me, I usually	— get defensive because I am expecting bad news — get excited because I expect good news — get nervous because I don't want to be embarrassed — don't look forward to it because it is often a waste of time — look forward to it because it is often useful
2. When someone tells me that I did something in a poor way, I usually	— immediately try to explain that there was a good reason for it — keep quiet and dismiss the criticism — ask questions for clarification — argue with the critic — write the comments down for later reference
3. When someone praises me saying I did a good job, I usually	— accept the praise, say thank you and smile — ask questions as to what was meant by "good job" — disagree with the critic and point out weaknesses to which he or she didn't refer
4. When I am asked to criticize others, I usually	— would rather not because I don't know enough — would rather not because I don't like saying bad things about people — look forward to giving my opinion — am very honest about what I like or don't like — am not very honest especially when it is something I don't like
5. When I am asked to criticize others' communications skills, I usually	— say whatever comes to mind at the time — am very frank — am a little vague — apply specific techniques I know for giving useful feedback

Many people do not like to receive or give criticism. They see it as a negative thing. For them, it is an occasion of tension, nervousness, and sometimes acute embarrassment. We often use the word criticize to mean "put down." But criticism should not be an attack. If the critic is simply demolishing, then the critic is not being effective. Criticism is a tool for getting better. First, criticism can help you understand what works well and what should be kept or repeated in future presentations. Second, it helps you identify what doesn't work well, helps you to get at the reasons why, and suggests ways you can improve. With this approach, even what might have previously been considered "negative criticism" is a helpful step to becoming a more effective presenter. You will be asked to both give and receive criticism. The people you criticize will in turn criticize you. If the presenter has the responsibility to research and give the best presentation, the listener has the responsibility to be just as thoughtful with the critique.

Actually, negative feedback is not the main problem encountered in speaking classes. The bigger problem is vague, unhelpful criticism. You know you have got that kind of feedback when you walk away without really knowing what to do next time around. You will be asked to fill out evaluation forms for your team members as they present. These forms appear in latter units. For now, consider the kind of criticism you would like to both receive and give in those forms.

Developing a Criticism Policy

Having completed your inventory of attitudes toward criticism, bring that understanding to a group discussion aimed at carving out what criticism should be now and especially for the formal presentations later. Think of it in terms of a policy statement. What is the purpose of criticism in a presentations class? How should it be conducted? What are the ground rules?

Getting the Most out of Criticism	TASK ONE

Person 2: Facilitate the discussion and be sure that everyone has a chance to contribute. After the discussion is finished, facilitate the wording of the policy statement.

Person 4: Record the results of the discussion in a notebook. Later, record the polished statement in the policy box.

Person 3: Be ready to read out your policy statement to the class if asked.

Person 1: Keep track of the time. You will be told how much time is devoted to this exercise.

Hint

First, think of the kind of critique that you would like to get from your group as you work through this book. Second, think of the kind of critique that you wouldn't want to get. One way to get at this is simply to ask yourself what would be helpful and what wouldn't be? The answers will be a guide for you in critiquing others.

POLICY STATEMENT FOR CRITICISM

Case Studies

You received each of the following sets of comments after a different presentation you gave. Discuss these comments with your group and identify how that criticism could have been improved. Does it follow the policy statement that your group just wrote? If it doesn't follow the policy, use the right column to rewrite some of the comments so that it does.

Case One

You have just given your first extended presentation to this class. The purpose was to acquaint your audience with something it did not know before. You collected several assessment sheets when you were done. The following comments appeared on various sheets.

Criticism	Should Be
Great job!	
Perfect!	
Good work.	
Fine for me.	

WHAT IS THE PROBLEM WITH THE COMMENTS IN CASE ONE?

_____

_____

_____

_____

Case Two

Having completed your first presentation in the class, you worked on a more challenging second presentation. This presentation required you to use specific examples, case studies, or anecdotes. You found some excellent examples that demonstrated your points perfectly. The students gave you the following criticism on the assessment forms.

Criticism	Should Be
Nobody could hear you.	
The class was bored with the topic.	
The students couldn't relate to your examples.	

WHAT IS THE PROBLEM WITH THE COMMENTS IN CASE TWO?

_____

_____

_____

_____

Case Three

You have just given a third presentation. The main requirement was to use visuals as you made your point. You opted for PowerPoint slides. Here is the feedback on the assessment sheets from your team members.

Criticism	Should Be
I didn't like the way you started the introduction. I thought some of your examples could have been clearer. I had trouble understanding the visual.	

WHAT IS THE PROBLEM WITH THE COMMENTS IN CASE THREE?

_____

_____

_____

_____

Case Four

You have just completed a more advanced presentation in the class. This presentation required extensive research on an important issue. You spent the last two weeks checking reference libraries and downloading documents from electronic databases. You found the following comments on the assessment sheets.

Criticism	Should Be
You didn't do enough research for this one. You didn't practise enough before you came. You are not interested in the subject yourself, so how could you expect us to be interested?	

WHAT IS THE PROBLEM WITH THE COMMENTS IN CASE FOUR?

_____

_____

_____

_____

Essential Elements of Giving Criticism

Use your analysis of the case studies and your identification of the problems in each one to complete the following form. What makes for effective criticism? What should it be?

CRITICISM SHOULD BE

1. _____

2. _____

3. _____

4. _____

TASK TWO   Advanced Criticism Skills

Part One

Your group has now developed a policy, analyzed cases, and identified at least four governing principles of effective criticism. Your task now is to expand that understanding. What is the difference between feedback and criticism? What other effective, specific techniques for giving criticism can you find? Think about these questions and consult as many sources as you can. These sources can include on-line documents, texts, or discussions with instructors who are, after all, in the critiquing business. Bring your results to the next group meeting.

Hint

Giving and taking criticism belong to interpersonal skills. Texts on psychology and human relations are useful sources in addition to texts on presentation skills.

Part Two

Person 3: Facilitate this discussion. Give every person an opportunity to present his or her findings. Invite comments or amendments from the group before the results are recorded.

Person 4: Record the results in the master list provided.

DIFFERENCE BETWEEN FEEDBACK AND CRITICISM

Feedback	Criticism

ADDITIONAL TECHNIQUES FOR GIVING EFFECTIVE CRITICISM

Part Three

Person 2: Rotate through the various groups presenting the results from your group's work on Task Two.

Remaining Group Members: Take notes of any ideas or techniques that are new to your group as you hear the various presentations.

Step Up and Present

Taking Criticism

Your group has discussed how to give criticism that will be concrete, constructive, honest, clear, and focused on specific, observable behaviour. The other side to all of this is what you do with the criticism you receive. Taking criticism requires just as much training as giving it.

Take a look at the following case studies. What is ineffective about the way the presenter takes criticism in each case? What would be a better response?

Case One

You have begun to point out to a presenter that you would have appreciated more background in the introductory material. You were planning to complete your comment by saying that the topic was totally new to you. The presenter steps in, however, to explain that most people know a little bit about the subject and that since there was a very tight time frame for the talk, it was better to cut the background out.

Problem	Better Response

Case Two

You have identified the features of a presentation you like. The presenter is smiling and nodding. She says, "thank you." You now begin to talk about improvements. You note that you had trouble hearing some of the points and that more attention to volume would help future presentations. You also note that you had to work a little at keeping your attention focused because of the monotone delivery and that you needed more voice colour to keep up your interest. Finally, you state that you were sometimes distracted by the presenter's fidgeting with a pen and that you would have enjoyed more directed gestures toward the visual instead. The presenter is no longer smiling, but looking away. Her face is flushed. When you finish, she picks up her papers and throws them on her desk and sits down folding her arms across her chest.

Problem	Better Response

Case Three

You begin to state that you needed a clearer visual to keep the stats and relationships straight. The presenter tells you that there was nothing wrong with the visual. It makes perfect sense to him. You explain that you had trouble finding the information while he spoke because there was too much text. In fact while you were trying to figure it out, you lost some of what he said. He tells you that your comment is ridiculous because you should have been paying attention. He had a visual with the necessary information and explained it clearly enough for anyone who had any listening skills. There is absolutely no need to do anything with the visual. He says that you should get over that and get on with your critique.

Problem	Better Response

Essential Elements of Taking Criticism

Use your analysis of the case studies and your identification of the problems in each one to complete the following form. Add any others your group identifies.

TAKING CRITICISM AND MAKING THE MOST OF IT MEANS

1. _____

2. _____

3. _____

In Summary

Take three minutes to write a summary of what you learned from participating in the tasks of Unit 4.

UNIT 5

Knowing Your Audience

Here's what you'll work on in this unit.

- Analyzing your audience
- Applying the rhetorical triangle to presentations
- Developing questions to assess your listeners
- Building a profile of an audience through surveying

One of the most important parts of preparation for any communication task is to size up your audience. If you are writing, you need to know your readership. If you are speaking, you need to know your audience. Every audience has a different profile. Some audiences might be supportive of what you have to say, others might not. Some audiences may be very interested in your subject, others may not. In some cases, your audience may share a great deal of background about your subject. In others cases, the audience may know very little.

The Importance of Knowing Your Audience

Why is knowing your audience so important? You want your communication task to succeed. If you attend a job interview, you want to get the job. If you are making a promotional presentation, you want the audience to buy what you're selling. If you design a one-size-fits-all presentation you will only succeed with a small portion of the audience, but the rest of it will find that its needs are not met. There is a key to all of this. A presenter who wants to give the most effective presentation possible needs to assess the needs of the audience. Recognizing and meeting the needs of the audience is a strong step in accomplishing your task. Do you want the audience to understand something? Then you need to assess what the listeners already know. If you start at a point above them, you will never be able to bring them to where you want to go. Do you want your audience to do something when you are finished your talk? Then you need to assess just how much commitment they already have to your topic.

You will find a number of tools available to help you assess your audience. This unit will ask you to work through some of them.

The Rhetorical Triangle

The rhetorical triangle method can be applied specifically to each of your presentation situations. It works like this. Each presentation has three elements: you, subject, and audience. When you put the elements on the points of a triangle, you can begin to see the relationships.

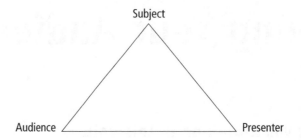

Figure 5.1

The first step in assessing your audience using this method is to consider the relationship on each side of the triangle. Here's a case and the results of that analysis.

Sample Case

You have a part-time position working for the college fitness club. The manager has asked you to make a presentation to students in your program about the club to drum up more memberships. Before you put your presentation together, you fill out the rhetorical triangle.

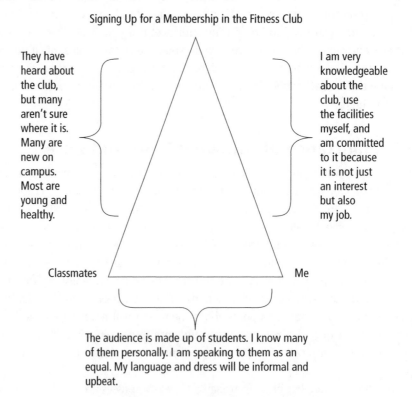

Figure 5.2

When you have completed the triangle, step back and work out what the needs of the audience are. In this case, you might decide upon the following.

Audience Need

The audience needs to know where the club is and what kind of facilities it has. Since the audience is young and generally healthy, it might find the club a good place to socialize, release the stress of study, body build, or generally improve their appearance.

Using the Rhetorical Triangle

TASK ONE

Part One

Apply the rhetorical triangle to the case described below.

Person 2: Facilitate the task and make sure everyone has an opportunity to comment.

Person 1: Record the results on the blank triangle provided.

Person 3: Keep track of the time. The group has 15 minutes for this activity.

Person 4: Be prepared to present your analysis to the class.

Case

You did such an excellent job getting memberships from students for the club that your boss has now set you another task. This time you are to attend a

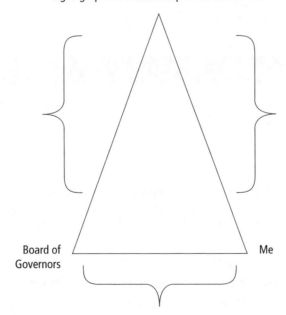

Signing Up for a Membership in the Fitness Club

Board of Governors

Me

Figure 5.3

board meeting for the Board of Governors of your college. You discover from your research that there will be 12 people present. Nine of them are men and three are women. Ages range from 55 to 63. You are number three on a seven point agenda at the meeting. You will have 10 minutes.

Step Up and Present

Part Two

Person 4: Explain to the class how your group would handle this presentation. What need would you focus on? What would you emphasize in your talk? What approach and style would you use?

The Audience Profile

The clearer you are about the relationships on the triangle, the better the handle you will have as to what you need to do in your presentation. If you don't already know your subject well, you need to research it before you present. The same thing goes for your audience. The clearer you are about your audience, the more accurate your analysis. In this book, you will address different topics to different specific audiences. When you are in other presentation situations, ask some questions beforehand. For example, it is important to know just how many people will be listening. You will want to get some sense of their familiarity with your subject. Are they there voluntarily or are they required to hear what you have to say? This kind of information will help you decide how receptive they likely will be and what kind of approach would be most suitable for them. You can ask these questions of whoever asked you to speak. In some cases, speakers visit the presentation site ahead of time to learn more about the people who will attend the presentation. Some presenters advocate using questionnaires to survey a group before going in to deliver. Consider ahead of time just what you would like to know about them.

TASK TWO	**Developing an Audience Profile**

This task asks you to consider what kind of information would be helpful in developing an audience profile.

Part One

Person 3: Lead the group and make sure everyone has an opportunity to speak. Ask the group to develop a checklist of the kinds of information that would be useful for each of the following cases.

Person 2: Record the results in the form provided.

Person 4: Keep track of the time. The group has 15 minutes.

Person 1: Read each of the cases to the group.

Case One

You are presenting an informative talk on the changing technology in your field.

USEFUL INFORMATION ABOUT THE AUDIENCE WOULD INCLUDE

_____

_____

_____

_____

_____

Case Two

You are instructing new hires in your company how to operate potentially dangerous equipment and troubleshoot using the accompanying manual.

USEFUL INFORMATION ABOUT THE AUDIENCE WOULD INCLUDE

_____

_____

_____

_____

_____

Case Three

You are an outside consultant running a sexual harassment seminar for a company at the employer's request.

USEFUL INFORMATION ABOUT THE AUDIENCE WOULD INCLUDE

_____

_____

_____

_____

_____

Case Four

You are presenting an argument around the ethics of cloning human beings. You are the guest speaker at a fundraising luncheon.

USEFUL INFORMATION ABOUT THE AUDIENCE WOULD INCLUDE

_____

_____

_____

_____

_____

_____

◁

The Audience Profile: Surveying

The information that you need for each of the cases above is important to help you determine the specific needs of that audience in that particular speaking occasion. Another way of developing a profile is surveying the audience directly beforehand. Whereas you can always ask questions of the organizer before you present, surveying the audience isn't something you can do very often. Where feasible, though, it can provide you a great deal of hard data to help you gauge just what your audience is thinking. Ask your audience short questions with definite answers that can be tabulated. When you survey your audience, avoid giving them the opportunity to opt for non-committal answers. For example, instead of asking the following:

Do you eat junk food?
- ❏ regularly
- ❏ sometimes
- ❏ never

it would be better to ask this:

Do you eat junk food?
- ❏ regularly
- ❏ often
- ❏ rarely
- ❏ never

The first question will likely give you a large number answering "sometimes," which isn't really very helpful because it is not clear what "sometimes" really means. Answers to the second question will give you a much clearer picture of the behaviour of that group. You now have something you can work with.

Developing a Class Profile TASK THREE

A speaker is coming to present a talk on a controversial subject to this class and asked for your help. She wants you to provide her with a profile of her audience. Develop a profile of this class to help her refine her talk.

Part One

Person 1: Lead the group and make sure everyone has an opportunity to speak. Ask the group to do the following:

- Identify a controversial subject upon which a visiting speaker will present. It can be a hot topic in the news, a social or political issue, or an issue at college.
- Fill out the profile form on page 46 for your class.
- Decide on whatever other information the speaker would like to have about the audience for this issue, and develop one or two survey questions. Those questions can go in the blank spots on the form.

Person 4: Record the results in the form provided.

Person 2: Keep track of the time. The group has 30 minutes.

Person 1: Be the messenger and questioner. Ask your class to respond to any questions your group added to the class profile.

Hint

You are already likely very familiar with your class. You can estimate the age range, count the numbers of women and men, and make any other observation that would help the speaker. If you have a specific question about the class that would help the profile, but to which you do not know the answer, send person 1 to the groups to get the necessary information.

CLASS PROFILE

Item	Specifics	Number/Response
Number of People	*Female*	
	Male	
Age Groups	*18–30*	
	31–40	
	41–50	
	51–60	
	61–70	
	71+	
Familiarity with the Issue	*Completely*	
	Very	
	Hardly	
	Not at all	

Step Up and Present

Part Two

Person 1: Announce the issue to the class, provide any definitions or background necessary, and present the results of your profile analysis.

With this information in hand, the presenter could now go on to plan an effective presentation that would take into account the audience's background and preferences. In this way, the presentation becomes focused on the listeners rather than on the speaker and has a much higher chance of success.

In Summary

Take three minutes to write a summary of what you learned from participating in the tasks of Unit 5.

Part 2

Delivery

A strong presentation depends in part on good research, clear organization, and solid content. It also depends on effective techniques for delivering that content. The units in Part 2 give you the opportunity to explore the different facets of delivering a strong presentation. You will reflect on successful presentations in order to determine just what you can do to be an effective presenter. In particular, you will identify and develop techniques for voice, movement, and the effective use of visuals. Units in this part will help you identify what presentation style is the most appropriate for your purposes, what kind of introduction would best fit your audience, and what kind of closing strategies you can employ.

UNIT 6

Effective and Ineffective Presentations

Here's what you'll work on in this unit.

- Reflecting on memorable presentations
- Identifying the features of effective presentations
- Evaluating your ability to present effectively
- Developing a list of personal priorities for successful presenting
- Solving ineffective presentation scenarios
- Reflecting on ineffective presentations you have attended
- Developing a list of what to avoid when giving presentations
- Analyzing a presentation you gave that you were not satisfied with
- Developing presentations for the class

What Makes a Strong Presentation?

Some presentations just stand out from all the rest. Whenever you see a great presenter in action, ask yourself just what it is that makes you say, "This is a great presentation." What is the speaker doing that you can learn to do as well? Sometimes, you will discover a little technique that is easy to incorporate into your style yet dramatically improves the effect of your presentation. At other times you will find that what another does just doesn't work for you at all. Rather than dismiss it altogether, though, you can adapt that method to your own unique style.

Reflecting on Successful Presentations

When you start to determine what it is that really makes a presentation work, think about why it works and just how you might be able to achieve the same results. Good eye contact, attention to movement, and varied voice colour are just three things that can help you deliver an effective presentation. There are many more to discover. Keep your own list as a set of targets for your presentations by the end of this book. Table 6.1 is an example of such a list.

TABLE 6.1 DELIVERY TIPS FOR AN EFFECTIVE PRESENTATION

Element	Reason (Why It Works)	Application (How It Works)	My Own Experience
Good eye contact with the audience	A personal approach is very successful with an audience. People like to be talked to, not talked at. People like to be acknowledged. Eye contact implies confidence in what you have to say. When you pay attention to your audience, your audience pays attention to you.	Avoid the temptation to work from a full text. It is just too easy to start reading it. The papers in your hand become a wall between you and your listeners. Decide to look at different people in each of the areas of your audience, no matter how small or large. If it is hard to do at first, find a few friendly faces or even look between people at different spots around the room.	— I can do that well. — I can do it only with effort and determination. It doesn't come naturally. — I really need to work on this one.
Animated delivery	Gestures help emphasize points and give the audience something to look at. Your presentation does not just depend upon your voice, but on your whole being. Moving around and using your hands not only gives you a channel for your nervous energy, it also helps create interest.	Directed actions, as opposed to fidgeting, grow out of the message you are giving. Until that comes naturally, you can plan certain moments to step towards your audience, point, or raise your hands. Decide what parts of your message are particularly important and need emphasis. Where would a movement of your hands describing a shape or position fit in?	— I can do that well. — I can do it only with effort and determination. It doesn't come naturally. — I really need to work on this one.

Element	Reason (Why It Works)	Application (How It Works)	My Own Experience
Voice colour	Voice colour is to your voice as movement is to your body. Audiences find it easier and more interesting to listen to a varied delivery. No matter how great your content might be, it will get lost in a flat monotone. Variety in voice colour means attention to changes in pitch (highs and lows), rate (fast and slow), and volume (loud and soft).	Voice colour is a feature of your delivery that will also develop naturally. It has nothing to do with accent. People with accents can deliver interesting varied talks, just as people without accents can deliver flat, monotone talks. Like gesture and movement, voice colour can be planned until it becomes automatic. What part of your message deserves a louder, higher tone for emphasis? What part of your message could be differentiated from the rest in a lower, quieter tone?	— I can do that well. — I can do it only with effort and determination. It doesn't come naturally. — I really need to work on this one.

TASK ONE Great Presentation Stories

Part One

Think about different presenters you have seen in your life: instructors in class, speakers at special events, hosts at weddings, clerics at religious ceremonies, and so many more. Which presenter stands out for you? What did the presenter do that made it so memorable? Why did it work? How was it done? Take five minutes to prepare your story about a memorable presenter to share with your group.

Person 2: Manage and coordinate this activity. Give everyone five minutes to prepare, and then be sure that everyone in the group has a chance to tell their story.

Person 3: Note down the effective elements shared by each person in the chart below using the chart above as a model. Don't worry about the column entitled My Own Experience for now.

Person 4: Please keep time for this activity, and give reminders to the group as to when it needs to move on.

DELIVERY TIPS FOR AN EFFECTIVE PRESENTATION

Element	Reason (Why It Works)	Application (How It Works)	My Own Experience
			— I can do that well. — I can do it only with effort and determination. It doesn't come naturally. — I really need to work on this one.
			— I can do that well. — I can do it only with effort and determination. It doesn't come naturally. — I really need to work on this one.
			— I can do that well. — I can do it only with effort and determination. It doesn't come naturally. — I really need to work on this one.
			— I can do that well. — I can do it only with effort and determination. It doesn't come naturally. — I really need to work on this one.

Element	Reason (Why It Works)	Application (How It Works)	My Own Experience
			— I can do that well. — I can do it only with effort and determination. It doesn't come naturally. — I really need to work on this one.
			— I can do that well. — I can do it only with effort and determination. It doesn't come naturally. — I really need to work on this one.

Part Two

Group members help person 3 organize a three to five minute presentation to the entire class. The subject is the top three skills and tips your group discovered aside from the ones mentioned in Table 6.1. The talk must explain each tip, how it worked in a particular presentation, and why it was so effective.

Hint

Choose the skills that come up more than once in the individual stories. Person 3 can summarize the stories connected with each rather than retell them.

Step Up and Present

Person 3: Deliver the talk. Use the three tips you are introducing as much as possible as you present.

Group members: Note down in your own Delivery Tips for an Effective Presentation list the ideas you get as you listen to the other presentations in the class.

Part One

Spend a few moments rereading the tips and check off the appropriate box in the My Own Experience column. Look over the column when you are done. Which of these tips for better presentations do you want to make your priority? It may be that you want to be able to check the "I can do that well" box off for all of them. It may be that some do not fit in with your own personal style. Whereas good eye contact is something everyone should aspire to, it is not the case that everyone needs to be adept at using humour in a presentation. Summarize what you are going to work on in the top box of the chart entitled Personal Priorities for Developing an Effective Presentation. Leave the bottom box blank for now. Photocopy that page and bring it in next class.

PERSONAL PRIORITIES FOR DEVELOPING AN EFFECTIVE PRESENTATION

Part Two

Briefly explain your personal priorities to the group, and put the sheet into the group portfolio. Your group members and instructor will use it to evaluate your progress later in the book. They will give you specific ideas on how you are doing as you work toward great presentation skills. That's what the bottom box is for. You will also do the same for the other members in your group. In this way, you will get concrete feedback on how effective a presenter you have become.

What Should You Avoid in a Presentation?

As a speaker, you will need to keep in touch with your audience and be sensitive to its reaction. The rhetorical triangle and audience profiling in Part One are methods to help you do just that. Another helpful technique is to think about your experience as part of an audience. Have you ever attended a presentation that just didn't work for you? If you have, what was your reaction? Many people just tune out. They allow themselves to become bored and turn their minds to other things. Did a speaker ever bore you? That's not the worst thing that can happen. Sometimes a speaker's inept presentation skills can make him or her look ridiculous. If that happens, the credibility of both the speaker and the message suffer.

Instead of giving in to boredom or just dismissing the message, it can be helpful to analyze a presentation like that. In that way, everything becomes useful. Good presentations are opportunities for you to pick up a technique or learn a new skill. Poor presentations become opportunities for reflection. It might be a student presentation or a faculty lecture. It might be a report at a meeting or a briefing at work. What went right? What could have gone better? What kind of solutions can you come up with to make a weak presentation stronger?

Here are some examples.

Case Studies

Read out the following case studies in your groups. What solutions can you recommend?

Case One

You are sitting in a class, one of 80 students. The desks are tight and close together. It's about halfway through term and you really need a reading week. The instructor is at the front of the class, sitting behind a desk. He has a sheaf of papers in front of him and is reading a lecture to you. When he looks up, he glances at the ceiling and then returns to his notes. People beside you are chatting in low voices. The instructor doesn't seem to notice or care. He just keeps going on in a monotone voice. Your mind has wandered a number of times and when you look at your binder, you discover less than half a page of notes. This just isn't working out. The instructor ends with a comment that some of his notes from this lecture are, as usual, posted online in a PowerPoint presentation. Later that night you sign in to check them out because you didn't get too much out of today's class. You are surprised as you go through the slides at how good this information really is. It is really helpful and well organized.

Analysis

The first thing that this case demonstrates is that there is a clear difference between content and packaging. Just because a presentation is dull, doesn't mean that the content is poor. It works the other way, too. Just because a presentation is brilliant, doesn't mean that the content really has a lot of substance. That is, after all, what many politicians rely upon. The next thing that stands out is that environment has a lot to do with a presentation. The overcrowded room, the uncomfortable seats, and the chatting neighbours all detracted from the presentation. The time of the academic year, particularly the upcoming reading week, didn't really predispose the students to want to be there in the first place. Many elements are beyond the control of a speaker and that's where good listening skills come in. Third, the speaker had distanced himself from his listeners by putting two barriers between them. The first barrier was the desk; the second barrier was that sheaf of papers that he would not look away from except to glance at the ceiling. As the audience became aware that the instructor was not going to even look at them, they stopped paying attention to him. That's when the conversations started. Finally, the lack of variety in the instructor's voice was a major problem. If he didn't seem excited or at least interested in the topic, why should the students have been?

Solutions

WHAT CAN THE SPEAKER REASONABLY DO TO MAKE THIS PRESENTATION MORE EFFECTIVE?

Case Two

It is presentation day in your class. A student gets up to begin the major persuasive presentation that everyone is required to give. The student rattles off an ordinary start: "Today, I am going to talk about ...." In fact, you remember that it is one of the starting methods that your class had discussed was not very effective. The presentation starts to meander and you begin having trouble understanding what she means. You ask yourself, What is the main point of this anyway? Several pauses and repetitions make you suspect that she actually doesn't have a main point. You find yourself distracted as she fingers a pen that she brought up with her but hasn't used for anything. This whole presentation is becoming uncomfortable for you to watch. You wish it would just end. Nothing much is coming out of it, and it is painful watching her squirm up there.

Analysis

Lack of preparation is a chief cause of poor presentations. Preparation means a number of things. The speaker needs to research the topic, plan the talk, prepare appropriate visuals when needed, and practise. Rehearsal, especially for beginning presenters, is essential. Until you rehearse, you're not entirely sure if your presentation fits your time frame or if it flows smoothly. The lack of preparation made the speaker in this case nervous. That nervousness came out through fidgeting, which distracted you. It also came out through a hesitant vocal delivery. Her pauses and stumbles gave away the fact that she really did not have much to say. Combine all this with a predictable opening and you had the makings of a presentation that was embarrassing for both the speaker and the listener.

Solutions

WHAT CAN THE SPEAKER REASONABLY DO TO MAKE THIS PRESENTATION MORE EFFECTIVE?

Reflecting on Ineffective Presentations

Looking at effective presentations is only one way to improve your own skills. Another useful method is to think about why an ineffective presentation didn't work and how it could have been better.

Ineffective Presentation Stories   TASK THREE

Person 3: Keep time for this exercise. Give the group a one-minute warning before time expires.

Part One

Take five minutes to jot down examples of poor presentations that you attended. These presentations can be from school, work, extra-curricular organizations, meetings, or just about anywhere.

Part Two

Take another five minutes and choose two examples in which you had different reactions. You might have been bored with one and uncomfortable with the other. Prepare to tell the stories to your team.

Part Three

Person 2: Manage this task. Invite everyone in the group to tell one of the prepared stories. Ask each person to select a story that is the most different from the other stories heard in the group.

Part Four

Person 2: Ask the group to choose one of the stories for analysis. Lead a 15 minute discussion as to what happened in the presentation. Identify the various elements that led to the reaction of the listener. How could that presenter have done things differently?

Person 1: Record the selected story and the analysis. Use the form provided.

Part Five

Group members assist person 4 to prepare a short presentation to the class on the case study that the group discussed. The challenge for this presentation is to actually duplicate as many of the problems in the story as possible in person 4's own presentation style.

Person 4: Present the case, the analysis, and solutions to the class. Be sure to duplicate some of the problems in the case in your own presentation.

Step Up and Present

The Situation

Problems	Solutions

As you listen to the presentations from each of the other groups and as you see the presenters deliberately employing the habits and problems of poor presentations, note down what things you should avoid in your own presentations in the future. Put the problems down in the left column. Make a note as to why they are problems in the middle column. What effect does each of the problems have on a listener? Finally, note down any solutions that you want to remember in the right hand column. What are some of the most interesting solutions to these problems that you would like to try out?

WHAT TO AVOID IN A PRESENTATION

Problem	Why It Is a Problem	Solutions

Do this task on your own. Think of a presentation you gave that you were not satisfied with. For the purpose of this exercise, choose the weakest presentation you can remember. It might have been a project that you presented in a classroom, an address you made at a social occasion, or a speaking event at work. Spend some time thinking about the presentation and fill out the analysis sheet below. This task is just for you. You don't need to share it with the rest of the group.

MY OWN INEFFECTIVE PRESENTATION

Situation

Why I Wasn't Satisfied	**Solutions**

Listener Reaction

Final Comments

In Summary

Take three minutes to write a summary of what you learned from participating in the tasks of Unit 6.

_____

_____

_____

_____

_____

_____

_____

_____

_____

_____

_____

_____

_____

_____

_____

_____

_____

_____

_____

_____

_____

_____

_____

UNIT 7

Presentation Styles

Here's what you'll work on in this unit.

- Identifying and using four different presentation styles
- Evaluating the advantages and disadvantages of each style
- Determining when each style is appropriate and not appropriate
- Participating in a panel discussion

Finding the Right Style

The presentations you have given so far have been short and informal. You will be asked to give longer, more formal presentations in upcoming units. Different presentation styles are available to you. Each has its particular advantages and disadvantages. Each is more appropriate in certain situations than others. Knowing each style and what it has to offer is critical for making the best choice for your own presentations.

TASK ONE   Using Presentation Styles

This task asks your group members to try out different presentation styles so that you can evaluate how they work and articulate when they would be appropriate. During the preparation phase of this task, work on your project privately and try not to look at the instructions for the other people in your group.

Please look at the directions for your number in Part One below.

Part One

Person 1: You have 15 minutes to prepare the following short presentation. Your task is to deliver the presentation by reading. You can go off somewhere to practise your delivery. When you present, remember to read the text. Do not attempt to memorize any part of it.

Immigration has become an important issue in Canada. In 1990, 214,230 immigrants came to Canada. That was an increase of 11.6 percent over the previous year. The largest group came from Hong Kong with a total of 13.7 percent, followed by immigrants from Poland at 7.7 percent. In 1995, Canada received 212,504 immigrants which was a decrease of 5.1 percent from the previous year. Immigrants from Hong Kong still accounted for the largest group at 14.9 percent, but the second largest group was now from India at 7.5 percent. Immigration levels rose in the new millennium. In 2002, Canada received 229,091 immigrants. The largest group of immigrants that year came from China at 14.51 percent. Immigrants from India constituted 12.58 percent. At the same time, the birth rate in Canada is declining. In fact, Statistics Canada reports that the 2002 birth rate was the lowest since it began to be recorded in 1921. In the last ten years, Canada's birth rate has dropped 25.4 percent. Whereas there were 1,715,900 children four years and under in 2001, projections indicate 1,640,200 in 2006. At the same time, Canada's senior population is growing dramatically, requiring a large working population to keep the social safety net healthy. It is clear that Canada, a country of immigrants founded on a welcoming immigration policy, needs to continue to welcome immigrants to contribute their talents and keep our population numbers strong.

Person 2: You have 15 minutes to prepare the following short presentation. Your task is to memorize the text below and deliver it without any notes. You can go off somewhere to practise your delivery.

Note: After the group comes back together, someone is going to ask, "What is my topic?" When you hear that question, answer, "Your topic is a national problem that needs fixing."

Hint

Memorize as much of the following text as possible in the time given to you. If you cannot memorize all of it, then give as much of the presentation word for word as possible without looking at your book. When you finish, indicate to the group that there was more, and summarize whatever you remember. It is key for this exercise, though, that you do not go back to the written words.

North Americans have become increasingly health conscious. Part of that awareness involves regular exercise. A great many exercise options have become standard as people search for the kind of physical activity that suits their particular needs. The most popular style in North America continues to be aerobic exercise. The aim of this exercise is to elevate the heart beat and keep it at that level for a prolonged period of time. Doctors recommend this approach to stave off heart disease, which is the number one killer in

Canada and the U.S. largely because of our fatty diets and sedentary life style. Aerobic exercise comes in many forms including jogging, stair climbing, and the use of equipment like exercise bikes or treadmills. Another exercise option, however, is a more gentle approach that emphasizes stretching and massage of internal organs. This style focuses on controlled breathing and slow movement. This style, too, comes in many forms including yoga and tai chi chuan. Practitioners develop flexibility and good circulation through this kind of exercise. Although a combination of both styles is ideal, people tend to gravitate to one style or another depending on personality, age, and other related factors.

Person 3: You have 15 minutes to prepare a 3-minute presentation. The subject is the material taught in a recent class you attended in any subject. Your task is to develop a set of point form notes that can fit in the following box. Be sure to present your points in the same order as they appear in your box. Refer to your points as you present, but do not attempt to read or memorize them.

Person 4: Go away for the next 15 minutes and take a break. When you return to the group, wait until person 3 has completed the presentation. When completed, ask the group the following question, "What is my topic?" Someone will answer your question. When you hear the answer, stand up and begin a three-minute presentation on that topic immediately. Do not take any time to prepare.

Part Two

Return to your group after the 15-minute preparation period. Begin the presentations in order of number.

Advantages and Disadvantages of Different Presentation Styles

You have just heard four different presentations in four different styles. The first style was reading. The second style was memorization. The third style was extemporaneous; that is, it depended on brief notes. The fourth style was impromptu; that is, there was no preparation and thus was presented "off-the-cuff." You will likely have encountered these various styles before. A political or religious leader might appear on television reading from a prepared text. A professor might deliver a lecture speaking freely on basic points in a PowerPoint presentation. A committee member might make a short presentation at a meeting on a point or issue that just came up. A contestant in a public speaking contest might deliver a memorized speech complete with prepared gestures. Different people and different texts promote different methods. The key to a good presentation is to find the style that delivers the particular advantages required in the situation. It is not that every presentation should be extemporaneous, or read, or memorized, or impromptu. The way to make that determination is to identify what advantages and disadvantages each brings.

Evaluating Presentation Styles	TASK TWO

This task asks you to evaluate the various presentation styles you have just experienced and then make some judgments as to when you might to use them.

Part One

Think about your experience with the presentation style you just used and fill out the form on page 68.

Part Two

Person 3: Facilitate this discussion. Ask each group member to tell the group what he or she liked about the presentation style assigned in the previous task. What was comfortable? What did he or she find problematic or difficult about that style? After each person has spoken, invite the other group members to add their observations, ideas, and opinions about the particular presentation style under discussion. Work through each of the four styles.

Person 4: On a blank piece of paper, record what the group identifies as the main advantages and disadvantages of each of the styles.

Presentation Style	
Advantages	**Disadvantages**

When Would You Use This Style?

When Would This Style Be Inappropriate?

Person 1: Keep track of the time. You will be told how much time is allotted for this task. Remind the group of how much time there is so that there is sufficient time to discuss each presentation.

Person 2: Be prepared to answer any questions about the group's findings in a panel discussion at the end of this activity.

Hint

Use the questions on the form as a guide for your group discussion.

Part Three

Person 2: Get together with all the other 2s in the class to form a panel. Be prepared to represent your group to answer questions and participate in a panel discussion on the advantages and disadvantages of the four presentation styles. The panel is moderated and led by the instructor. Here are some questions to consider.

- Did the group generally prefer any one style as the most effective for most situations?
- Did the group decide that any one style should be generally avoided?
- Was there any disagreement in the group over the advantages and disadvantages of any of the styles?
- Is any one style more risky than the others?

In Summary

Take three minutes to write a summary of what you learned from participating in the tasks of Unit 7.

UNIT 8

Starting and Ending

Here's what you'll work on in this unit.

- Identifying what to avoid in an introduction
- Developing ways to get listener interest
- Determining appropriate background for the subject
- Communicating relevance
- Establishing presenter credibility
- Clarifying purpose
- Writing complete introductions
- Determining what to avoid in a conclusion
- Developing strategies to end a presentation
- Identifying different types of conclusions
- Evaluating additional considerations including signaling, timing, and delivering on the promise
- Employing alternative concluding strategies for the same subject

Starting

As important as every part of your presentation is, the beginning deserves special attention. If you engage the listeners right from the start so that they want to hear more, then you have already gone a long way to ensuring the presentation will be successful. If, on the other hand, you do not engage the listeners up front, but, rather, bore or even antagonize them, you will have an uphill battle. You have lost precious time, which now must be spent bringing your audience back rather than moving on. Even if you manage to turn the presentation around and eventually capture the audience's interest, your presentation will have been much less effective than if you had grabbed the audience's attention right from the beginning.

The question is, though, just how do you do that? It is not so much a matter of the research and organization so necessary in the rest of the talk. It is more a matter of audience analysis, planning, and to a certain extent, intuition. You already know how to do audience analysis. That will help you know what the audience needs to hear and the style in which they should hear it. It will also help you select a strategy for kicking off the talk. Different methods are available, but don't just pick any one. Match the strategy to the audience and to what the presentation is trying to accomplish. Planning involves thinking about how the introduction can best serve the audience. Aside from a strategy to engage them, what does the introduction need to provide? Finally, over time you will develop an intuition as to what will work and what won't work for a particular group on a particular day. That has to do with being a flexible presenter. You may have a plan for the introduction and an outline for the talk, but as you become an experienced presenter, you will be able to "present on your feet" and vary the opening as you respond to the environment and the reactions of the audience.

Hint

One way of making your introductions even more effective is to wait until you have developed your entire presentation before considering what you will do in the introduction. In that way, you can ensure that the introduction connects well to the content.

What an Introduction Shouldn't Have

Looking at flawed introductions can help you determine effective strategies for starting a presentation.

It Could Be Better   TASK ONE

You will hear four openings to a talk. Please listen, rather than follow along in your text. Each one has one or more major flaws that require revision. After you hear the talk, tell the group what you think the problems are. Record the results below.

Person 1:   Read the following introduction.
I'm sorry I didn't find any pictures to bring you, but I think I can describe the construction of Toronto's CN Tower anyway. You probably have been up to the top yourself, so I won't talk about the great things inside. So, here goes.

PROBLEMS:

_____

_____

_____

_____

_____

Person 2:   Read the following introduction.

Today I am going to talk about mosquitoes. I learned about them last night as I got this talk ready. The Internet has a lot of material on them, and I am going to tell you some of what I found. You probably aren't that interested in mosquitoes, but after looking at the sites, I sure want to learn more.

PROBLEMS:

_____

_____

_____

_____

_____

Person 3:   Read the following introduction.

Question: What's frightening and stuck on the end of your arm?
Answer: A terror wrist.

But seriously, international terrorism has become a big problem that I would like to talk about with you. You never know if you might be blown up before you get home tonight.

PROBLEMS:

_____

_____

_____

_____

_____

Person 4:   Read the following introduction.

I am sure you want to get out of here as much as I do, so I will make this quick. Just because we have to learn this stuff, we don't have to drag it out—so you'll get the boiled down version. You probably know it all anyway. Here it is in a nutshell. I am going to talk to you about safety on this job site.

PROBLEMS:

What an Introduction Should Have

You have identified what an introduction should not have. Knowing what you want to avoid, you can then focus on the elements that the introduction should have. This unit will ask you to work on different components that work together to make effective openings to any presentation. These elements are the *hook, necessary background, relevance, credibility,* and *purpose.*

The Hook

The hook is an opening strategy that is aimed at grabbing the audience right at the start. Choose a strategy that is likely to make the audience want to listen to the next part of the presentation. Many inexperienced presenters begin with openings like, "Today I am going to talk about ...." With a little thought, they can replace an ordinary opening like that with an arresting start that startles, intrigues, or captivates the audience in some way. Several possibilities are open to you.

Identifying the Hook   TASK TWO

Part One

You will hear four different openings. Listen rather than follow along in your text. After you hear each one, identify what the speaker is doing to attract audience interest. Discuss the method with the group. How does it work?

Person 1: Read the following opening.

I'd like a show of hands. How many of you in this room have ever directly experienced racism of any kind? That's interesting. Keep your hands up. Take a look around and see who has their hands up. Are you surprised at how many hands you see? We might think that we are living in an enlightened society, but if that is true, why do we have this kind of response?

Method
How It Works

Person 2: Read the following opening.

True story. If you go to downtown King City north of Toronto, you will find an IGA grocery store. One day, just last year, a young man was crossing the street right in front of it. It was the middle of the day. Suddenly, without warning, a car careened around the corner. It seemed to come from nowhere. The car struck the young man who bounced off the hood. When the paramedics came, he was in a coma. He is still in a coma today. The driver of the car was drunk. Drunk driving has become too serious and too dangerous to ignore.

Method
How It Works

Person 3: Read the following opening.

Take the stone from the Great Pyramid in Egypt and you could build a wall that would completely encircle France. That's just one of the marvels of this incredible structure. There are many, many more.

Method	
How It Works	

Person 4: Read the following opening.

Chairman Mao Tse-Tung was right when he said, "political power comes from the barrel of a gun." Take a look at any news broadcast on any day. Take a look at any newspaper. Political power in our world is not so much a civilized process of debate, but rather a violent struggle. Even countries that use democratic processes still must rely on the military to keep those processes going.

Method	
How It Works	

Part Two

Person 2: Facilitate this task. Read the instructions below and give everyone a chance to contribute.

You have identified four types of hooks to use at the beginning of a presentation. What other ways of getting audience attention can you think of? Write the first four types in the table on page 76 and then add whatever new ones the group comes up with. Explain why these new hooks would work.

Person 1: Record the findings in the table provided.

Person 3: Keep time for the group. You have 20 minutes.

Person 4: Be prepared to present the group's findings.

Hint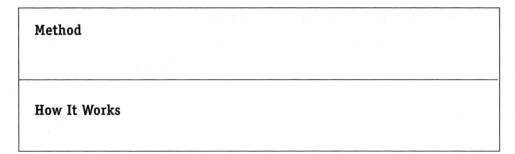

Think of any presentation that you have seen that was particularly memorable. How did the presenter begin? What was the most striking or effective way of starting of talk that you have encountered?

STRATEGIES FOR BEGINNING A PRESENTATION

	Type	Why It Works
1.		
2.		
3.		
4.		
5.		
6.		
7.		
8.		
9.		
10.		

Step Up and Present

Person 4: Leave your group and go to another group to present your list of opening strategies.

Person 1: Record any new strategies that your group hears.

Necessary Background Information

Another important element of the introduction is necessary background information. You don't have to provide all the background there is on a subject. Your audience would likely find it tedious if you did that. On the other hand, you do need to think about what your listener is likely to need to be able to understand your purpose and your main message. That information is the necessary background. What are necessary changes from audience to audience? The idea here is to give neither too little nor too much.

Person 4: Facilitate this task. Read the instructions below to the group.

The group chooses an aspect of your field that you have already studied in your program. Your task is to explain that topic to the specific audiences listed below. Each person outlines what kind of background would be needed for a particular audience and explains the decision to the group. Group members can propose modifications after each person presents.

Person 1: Your listener is a client.

NECESSARY BACKGROUND FOR THIS LISTENER INCLUDES

_____

_____

_____

_____

_____

Person 2: Your listener is senior management of the organization.

NECESSARY BACKGROUND FOR THIS LISTENER INCLUDES

_____

_____

_____

_____

_____

Person 3: Your listener is a colleague.

NECESSARY BACKGROUND FOR THIS LISTENER INCLUDES

_____

_____

_____

_____

_____

Person 4: Your listener is a student from another department.

NECESSARY BACKGROUND FOR THIS LISTENER INCLUDES

_____

_____

Relevance

Now that you have hooked the audience and given it enough information to understand just what it is you are going to talk about, give it a clear motivation for continuing to listen. Listeners will consciously or unconsciously ask themselves why they should give their time and energy to you. Settle that question for them in the introduction, and they will be more open to your presentation. If you can motivate them to listen for something particularly useful, they will actually work at paying attention and relating the content of your talk to themselves. If you have analyzed the audience using the rhetorical triangle presented in Unit 5, then you already know just what this audience needs. Here are some ways you can establish relevance.

- State what benefit the listener can gain.
- Highlight any serious problem that the listener can avoid.
- Make the relevance statement "you"-centred.
- Tell the audience that practical information for each person is in your presentation.

Here are some examples:

- By following these easy instructions you will save yourself hundreds of dollars, know that the job was done right, and develop self-confidence.
- You will know which diet plan is right for your body type by the end of this presentation.
- You will better understand the reasons for the Mideast conflict and how it affects you day to day.
- You can avoid a serious injury if you use your safety equipment in the way I am about to demonstrate.

Credibility

A good presenter anticipates questions. When you demonstrate the relevance of the talk to your listeners, you explain why they should care. Another question that they are likely to ask is, Does the presenter know what he or she is talking about? Can they trust your authority on the subject? If you make no reference to your background with the material, you lose a chance to create some confidence with your audience. You can establish your credibility in a number of ways.

- Make explicit any direct experience that you have with the subject.
- Tell the audience any expertise that you have.
- Refer to some of your sources.
- Demonstrate that you have spent considerable time working on the subject.

Here are some examples:

- I was in high school in Iraq when the war started. I saw it first hand.
- I have been studying Fitness and Lifestyle Management at college for the past two years. The dangers of fad diets have become an important part of the curriculum.
- Much of what I have to say comes from two studies, one by Dr. Rosenthal in Vancouver of 130 patients, and the other by Dr. Mackenzie in Los Angeles of 123 patients.
- I became interested in stress reduction over a year ago when I noticed just how many of my colleagues were overworked. Since then, I have examined the literature and investigated many stress reduction techniques.

Purpose

Finally, make your purpose crystal clear. Is your purpose to instruct? Make it clear to the audience that you are teaching and demonstrating how to do something. Is your purpose to inform? Tell your audience that the presentation will help them understand something that they need to know. Is your purpose to persuade? Make it clear to the audience that you have a point of view that you will demonstrate is valid.

Putting It All Together

TASK FOUR

This task asks you to put all the different elements of an introduction together for specific subjects to specific audiences.

Part One

Person 3: Facilitate this task. Read the instructions below and make sure everyone has an opportunity to contribute.

A speaker finished preparing four presentations on four topics to different audiences. These presentations now need introductions. Your job is to compose the full text of each. As a group, decide what the hook, necessary background, relevance statement, credibility statement, and purpose should be. The person whose number is on the presentation scenario records the group consensus in the sections below.

Person 2: Keep time. The group has 20 minutes to complete the task.

Presentation 1

The presenter is a student speaking at an open forum in a college about tuition fees.

HOOK:

_____

_____

_____

NECESSARY BACKGROUND:

_____

_____

_____

RELEVANCE:

_____

_____

_____

CREDIBILITY:

_____

_____

_____

PURPOSE:

_____

_____

_____

Presentation 2

The presenter is a car enthusiast running a seminar at a community centre on how to do an oil change and basic maintenance.

HOOK:

_____

_____

_____

NECESSARY BACKGROUND:

_____

_____

_____

RELEVANCE:

_____
_____
_____

CREDIBILITY:

_____
_____
_____

PURPOSE:

_____
_____
_____

Presentation 3

You are an immigrant to Canada who has been invited to speak to a church group about what the immigration process is like.

HOOK:

_____
_____
_____

NECESSARY BACKGROUND:

_____
_____
_____

RELEVANCE:

_____
_____
_____

CREDIBILITY:

_____

_____

_____

PURPOSE:

_____

_____

_____

Presentation 4

You are just about to graduate from your program. You have been invited by a local high school to talk about post-secondary education.

HOOK:

_____

_____

_____

NECESSARY BACKGROUND:

_____

_____

_____

RELEVANCE:

_____

_____

_____

CREDIBILITY:

_____

_____

_____

_____

_____

_____

Part Two

Take 10 minutes to write up the complete text of your introduction.

Part Three

Everyone presents his or her introduction in order of number. Give feedback to each person after the presentation is done.

Step Up and Present

▷

Ending

It is amazing what happens when a speaker says the magic phrase, "In conclusion...." Suddenly, people in the audience begin to sit up a little more in their chairs. Eyes turn to the presenter, ears tune in, and hands poise over notebooks to write something down. The audience might have been drifting, but somehow it hears the presenter announce that the talk is coming into the final stretch. Effective presenters know that the ending, like the introduction, is a key part of their presentations. A well-prepared introduction can grab attention and carry listeners well into the body of the talk. A well-prepared conclusion can leave a lasting message and make a strong impression. It is not something to be wasted or undervalued. Just as you employed techniques for your introduction, you can also develop methods to put together honed conclusions that will clinch your presentation.

What a Conclusion Shouldn't Have

It Could Be Better

TASK FIVE

You will hear four endings to a talk. Please listen, rather than following along in your text. Each one has one or more major flaws that require revision. After you hear the talk, tell the group what you think the problems are. Record the results below.

Person 1: Read the following conclusion.

So, I guess that's pretty well it about the CN Tower. Questions?

PROBLEMS:

_____

_____

_____

_____

_____

_____

_____

Person 2: Read the following conclusion.

So, as you can see, it is really important to protect yourself from mosquitoes. A little prevention can save you a lot of heartache.... There's another way to protect yourself aside from the ones I've mentioned. Don't wear any perfumes, colognes, or aftershave lotions. That's definitely something you don't want to do.

PROBLEMS:

_____

_____

_____

_____

_____

_____

Person 3: Read the following conclusion.

Terrorism is a serious issue. It has serious root causes like the ones we have just discussed: poverty, power struggles, and social injustice. Terrorism affects everyone in this room. Terror is a weapon that will likely be with us for a long time. But remember to always look on the bright side of life. The world is a beautiful place and you can enjoy it to the full.

PROBLEMS:

_____

_____

_____

_____

_____

_____

Person 4: Read the following conclusion.

I am sorry for having taken this long, and if my PowerPoint presentation had worked you might have got a better idea of workplace hazards, but if you follow these six basic workplace rules, you can help make this a safe working environment for you and your colleagues.

PROBLEMS:

_____

_____

_____

_____

_____

_____

▷

What a Conclusion Should Have

You have just looked at four ineffective conclusions. Each of them misses a valuable opportunity at the end of the presentation. The listeners are likely alert and ready for a message that they can take away. Put yourself in the place of the listener at one of your talks. Consider what you would want the presenter to do for you in the conclusion. You can more fully take advantage of that opportunity by employing one or more concluding techniques. These techniques include summarizing, appealing, linking, questioning, and predicting. Vary your concluding techniques from presentation to presentation to see which one works best for you.

Hint

Develop your introduction and conclusion together after you have planned out the body of your presentation. In that way, they will coordinate well and be geared to the main matter of your talk.

Summarizing

The conclusion is an opportunity for you to restate your key points. This technique is particularly useful in a long presentation. It allows you to connect the dots from one main point to another separate from the supporting detail in the body. If you carefully coordinate it to an introduction that announces ahead of time where the presentation is going, then the listener will hear the plan for the talk, the main points with support, and then a recapitulation of those points at the end. This method reinforces listener memory and makes sure that vital points aren't missed.

Appealing

An appeal is a personal connection with each member of your audience. After having demonstrated the value of your message, you ask each listener to get involved. It is a call to some kind of action that asks the listener to make a commitment. Just by thinking whether or not to make that commitment, the listener has engaged both you and your topic. It moves the listener from passivity to action. If you are speaking to an audience that is largely already onside with what you are saying, you can strengthen that appeal by turning it into a challenge. You can ask an audience to do more than pay lip service to a belief or value. You can encourage the listeners to set goals for themselves to reach.

Linking

Your conclusion can link back to what you did in the introduction. If you told a story at the beginning, you can add an extra note to that same story in the conclusion. If you started off with a striking fact, you could return to that fact at the finish. When you link in this way, you signal the listener that your presentation is wrapping up. It shows evidence of planning and ties up the presentation neatly. In other words, linking brings the presentation home.

Questioning

Your presentation does not have to have all the answers to a subject. It may be that you are opening a brand new area for the listener. The conclusion can end by posing some open-ended questions designed to keep the listener thinking about what you have said. These questions will likely stay in the listener's mind after the presentation has ended and can prompt further investigation.

Predicting

You can predict the outcome of a situation. Tell the listeners what will happen if they take action or don't take the action you recommend. Prediction is not new information but rather grows out of what you have already presented. Your conclusion can hold out alternative possibilities for the audience to consider. In that way, you leave strong, concrete images for people to take away and think about.

TASK SIX   Identifying the Concluding Strategy

Part One

You will hear four different endings. Please listen rather than follow along in your text. After you hear each one, identify what the speaker is doing to wrap up the presentation. Discuss the method with the group. How does it work?

Person 1:   Read the following closing.

That's what is still going on in our workplaces. If you feel strongly about racism, no matter how subtle it might be, then make it your business to find out about it. Don't let your education stop with this presentation. If you want to change things, then stand up when you see it in action. Name it for what it is, say that it is wrong, and refuse to have anything to do with it. Racism is not a problem for someone else to solve. The solution lies with me and with you.

Method
How It Works

Person 2: Read the following closing.

At the beginning of this presentation on drunk driving, I told you a story about a young man who was hit by a drunk driver while crossing the street in King City. Well, that young man is my brother and he is still in a coma today. That's why I'm giving this talk. It's for Roby's sake.

Method
How It Works

Person 3: Read the following closing.

These are the marvels of the Great Pyramid. The mathematical precision, the movement of tons of stone without the use of the wheel, the astronomical connections, and the engineering without the use of cranes testify to the genius of the ancients. Before modern people get too proud of their progress and technology and look down on the primitive civilizations of ancient times, they might want to just think about the pyramids.

<table>
<tr><td>**Method**</td></tr>
<tr><td>**How It Works**</td></tr>
</table>

Person 4:   Read the following closing.

If we don't treasure, use, and protect our democratic processes, we could easily lose them. We could find ourselves ruled by force in a totalitarian regime that has taken power because the people just didn't care enough. But if that's not what we want, if we hold onto our rights and responsibilities as citizens, if we fully engage ourselves in the political processes of our country and of our community, then we will see a flourishing democratic system that works for the good of everyone.

<table>
<tr><td>**Method**</td></tr>
<tr><td>**How It Works**</td></tr>
</table>

Part Two

Person 4:   Facilitate this task. Read the instructions below and give everyone a chance to contribute.

You have identified several types of concluding strategies to use at the end of a presentation. What other ways of ending can you think of? Write in the table on page 89 the different types already identified, then add whatever new ones the group comes up with. Explain why your new ending strategies would work.

Person 1:   Record the findings in the table provided.

Person 3:   Keep time for the group. You have 20 minutes.

Person 4:   Be prepared to present the group's findings.

STRATEGIES FOR ENDING A PRESENTATION

	Type	Why It Works
1.		
2.		
3.		
4.		
5.		
6.		
7.		
8.		
9.		
10.		

Part Three

Person 1: Leave your group and go to another group to present your list of closing strategies.

Person 3: Record any new strategies that your group hears.

Step Up and Present

Additional Considerations

Signaling

After choosing a particular strategy to end your presentation, decide whether or not you are going to overtly signal the end to the listener. If you are using the Linking technique, you may decide it is not necessary. The fact that you have returned to your opening example, story, or fact has already alerted the listener that you are wrapping things up. On the other hand, if you think that the audience may not be aware that you have left the body of the presentation, you might decide to signal that by saying," So, to conclude ..." or "Let's summarize all of this ..." or simply, "Finally...." Some speakers do not like to signal but prefer a smooth transition into the concluding paragraph. Try different styles in your upcoming talks and see which ones you prefer.

Timing

Another consideration is timing. Rehearse any presentation you are planning to give to be sure that it fits in the given time slot. Many speakers are tempted to shortchange the introduction and the conclusion so that they can get more points into the body or show an extra visual. Shortchanging the conclusion does not really pay off. Your audience is more likely to remember your conclusion than the extra point you put in the presentation. If the presentation seems rushed, abrupt, or in any way unsatisfying, that's the impression that will remain with the audience.

Delivering on the Promise

Ask yourself whether or not the presentation has accomplished its purpose. Did it deliver what it promised to deliver when you presented the purpose in the introduction? You can make that explicit in your conclusion by highlighting just what has been accomplished in your time with the audience.

TASK SEVEN   Putting It All Together

This task asks you to put all the different elements of a conclusion together for specific subjects to specific audiences.

Part One

Person 1:   Facilitate this task. Read the instructions below and make sure everyone has an opportunity to contribute.

Ask each person in the group to reread the introduction he or she wrote for a specific speaking situation. When they have finished reading, instruct them to write two different conclusions for the same presentation.

Person 3:   Keep time. The group has 20 minutes to complete the task.

Presentation 1

The presenter is a student speaking at an open forum in a college about tuition fees.

Conclusion 1

CONCLUDING STRATEGY:

FULL TEXT OF THE CONCLUSION:

Conclusion 2

CONCLUDING STRATEGY:

_____

FULL TEXT OF THE CONCLUSION:

_____
_____
_____
_____
_____

Presentation 2

The presenter is a car enthusiast running a seminar at a community centre on how to do an oil change and basic maintenance.

Conclusion 1

CONCLUDING STRATEGY:

_____

FULL TEXT OF THE CONCLUSION:

_____
_____
_____
_____
_____

Conclusion 2

CONCLUDING STRATEGY:

_____

FULL TEXT OF THE CONCLUSION:

_____
_____
_____
_____
_____

Presentation 3

You are an immigrant to Canada who has been invited to speak to a church group about what the immigration process is like.

Conclusion 1

CONCLUDING STRATEGY:

_____

FULL TEXT OF THE CONCLUSION:

_____
_____
_____
_____
_____

Conclusion 2

CONCLUDING STRATEGY:

_____

FULL TEXT OF THE CONCLUSION:

_____
_____

_____

Presentation 4

You are just about to graduate from your program. You have been invited by a local high school to talk about post-secondary education.

Conclusion 1

CONCLUDING STRATEGY:

_____

FULL TEXT OF THE CONCLUSION:

_____

_____

_____

_____

_____

Conclusion 2

CONCLUDING STRATEGY:

_____

FULL TEXT OF THE CONCLUSION:

_____

_____

_____

_____

_____

Part Two

Everyone presents his or her conclusions in order of number. Give feedback to each person after the presentation is done as to which conclusion you prefer and why.

Part Three

Person 2:   Coordinate the following task.

Ask each person to leave the group to meet a person with the same number in another group. Once there, they read out their conclusions to each other. Ask them to consider what changes they might make after hearing the alternative conclusions.

◁

In Summary

Take three minutes to write a summary of what you learned from participating in the tasks of Unit 8.

_____

_____

_____

_____

_____

_____

_____

_____

_____

_____

_____

_____

_____

_____

_____

_____

_____

UNIT 9

Using Your Voice

Here's what you'll work on in this unit.

- Defining voice colour
- Employing variations in pitch
- Employing variations in rate
- Employing variations in volume
- Marking a text for vocal delivery
- Determining problems with clarity
- Identifying the relationship between clarity and usage
- Identifying the relationship between clarity and enunciation

The effective delivery of a presentation is essential to its success. You might have the best message in the world, but if it isn't delivered in a way that really sticks with the audience, it can go by unappreciated or even ignored. We live in a world that has refined packaging so well that it is often the packaging, rather than the contents, that sells. Of course this is all problematic, but it is the reality. Does the most competent politician with the best ideas end up being elected? Sometimes, but all too often the best communicator, rather than the best thinker, gets the votes. Does the best person for the job end up getting hired? Sometimes, but all too often someone who isn't the most competent but has superior interview skills gets the offer. It is important that you have a strong, clear message that you believe in. But that isn't enough. You also need to be able to deliver that message in a way and in a style that hits home. This unit will ask you to think about what you can do vocally to give the most effective presentation possible.

Voice Colour

This book will use the term "voice colour" to describe an aspect of oral delivery. A painter has a wide range of colours to use to make vivid statements. These colours can complement each other for harmony and then, suddenly, contrast for striking emphasis. Your voice can do the same sort of thing for your message. You have a wide range of choices to make that can sometimes work together to enhance your point or contrast to make a point stand out that might otherwise be missed. Not all points carry equal weight in your argument. Voice colour is the key to helping your audience differentiate between major and minor points. Voice colour can also be a tool that makes sure that if your audience hasn't taken in everything you said, it will at least take away what you consider to be essential.

Hint

Another term for voice colour is voice dynamics. Some interesting Web sites on the subject are http://www.abacon.com/pubspeak/deliver/dynamics.html and http://www.uiowa.edu/~c100298/anxiety.html

---

TASK ONE   Identifying the Elements of Voice Colour

This task asks your group to read the same passage a number of different ways to identify the elements of voice colour and to determine just how important each is to the effective communication of a message. You will need three different colours of highlighters or pens to finish Part Three of this task.

Part One

Listen to person 1. Do not read along as person 1 presents.

Person 1:   Read the following passage to your group in as flat a manner as possible. Use a monotone, keep the speed exactly the same, and avoid any emphasis so that each word carries the same weight as all the others. When you finish, ask person 2 to read and carry out the next set of instructions.

> We know from the World Health Organization that over three million children in developing countries die each year from being underweight. In developed countries, obesity is one of the leading causes of death. More than one-third of all disease in those countries results from overweight, which causes high blood pressure and high cholesterol levels. Alcohol and tobacco use compound the problem. These contribute to the primary killer in developed countries, cardio-vascular disease. While people in developing countries die from malnutrition, more than 4 million people die each year in developed countries from high cholesterol, almost 5 million from tobacco use, and an incredible 7 million die from high blood pressure. What can we do about this? What can you do about this? First, start with yourself. Pay attention to your diet and stress factors. Check your blood pressure regularly. Get into good exercise and diet habits. Second, develop a global awareness. Respond generously to appeals for food aid to developing countries. Third, consider contributing your time to an organization that helps these people or even volunteer to work in developing countries to make life better for others who have so little.
>
> Source: *The World Health Report 2002*, Available at: http://www.who.int/whr/2002/overview/en/

Person 2: Read the same passage to the group, but use as many levels in pitch as possible. Sometimes raise your voice and sometimes lower your voice. Do this as naturally as possible. Do not, however, change the speed or volume. The volume of high-pitched words should be the same as that of the low-pitched words. Do not use volume to emphasize any particular word or phrase. The speed should be constant throughout. When you are done, ask person 3 to carry out the next set of instructions.

Person 3: Read the same passage to the group, but use as many changes in speed as possible. Sometimes speed up the reading. At other times, slow it right down. You can even stop and pause at certain places for effect. Do not, however, change your pitch or volume for emphasis. When you are done, ask person 4 to carry out the next set of instructions.

Person 4: Read out the passage one more time, but use as many changes in volume as possible. Sometimes lower your volume, but at other times increase the volume. Use volume to emphasis certain words or phrases for effect. Do not, however, change your pitch or speed. Keep both of those elements constant.

Part Two

Your group has just worked with three elements of voice colour: pitch, rate, and volume. Spend some time discussing how it felt to deliver the presentation and what it was like listening to it.

Person 4: Facilitate this task. Ask each person who gave the presentation to speak first about what it was like giving the presentation in that manner. If the person applied one of the elements, how did he or she choose when and what to do? When each person is finished, give the others a chance to comment on how the presentation sounded.

Person 1: Record the results in the table provided on page 98.

Part Three

This time, mark up the passage in your own books using a highlighter or coloured pen. You will find directions for each group member below. When you finish, bring your passage to person 1, who will compile the passages into a single copy.

Person 2: Use a coloured pen or highlighter to indicate on the text below when, in your judgment, the pitch should change and whether it should go up or down. Indicate how high or how low the pitch should be for either a particular word or a phrase. Take your text to person 1 when you are finished. Be prepared to explain your markings.

Person 3: Use a coloured pen or highlighter to indicate on the text below when, in your judgment, the speed should change and whether it should increase or decrease. Indicate how quickly or how slowly a phrase or sentence should be read. Indicate, too, when

Person and Element	Delivering the Presentation	Listening to the Presentation
Person 1: Flat		
Person 2: Pitch		
Person 3: Rate		
Person 4: Volume		

the reader should stop altogether for a pause. Take your text to person 1 when you are finished. Be prepared to explain your markings.

Person 4: Use a coloured pen or highlighter to indicate on the text below when, in your judgment, the volume should change and whether it should go up or down. Indicate how loud or how soft the speaker's voice should be for either a particular word or a phrase. Take your text to person 1 when you are finished. Be prepared to explain your markings.

We know from the World Health Organization that over three million children in developing countries die each year from being underweight. In developed countries, obesity is one of the leading causes of death. More than one-third of all disease in those countries results from overweight, which causes high blood pressure and high cholesterol levels. Alcohol and tobacco use compound the problem. These contribute to the primary killer in developed countries, cardio-vascular disease. While people in developing countries die from malnutrition, more than 4 million people die each year in developed countries from high cholesterol, almost 5 million from tobacco use, and an incredible 7 million die from high blood pressure. What can we do about this? What can you do about this? First, start with yourself. Pay attention to your diet and stress factors. Check your blood pressure regularly. Get into good exercise and diet habits. Second, develop a global awareness. Respond generously to appeals for food aid to developing countries. Third, consider contributing your time to an organization that helps these people or even volunteer to work in developing countries to make life better for others who have so little.

Person 1: Wait for each person to submit his or her text. Use a different colour for each person and transcribe that person's delivery decisions onto your master copy. Clarify with the person just exactly what is meant by the markings so that you work out a clear system.

Part Four

Take a look at the final text with your group's markings. Do any of the items overlap in the same places? Are there any points in the text where only one of the elements has been indicated? Are there particular passages that have no markings at all? What do the markings indicate about how these three elements of voice colour can be used to strengthen the delivery of a text?

Person 1: Take your master copy and go to another group. Read the text to this new group as your group members have directed. When you finish, go to a different group and read the text again.

Persons 2, 3, and 4: Listen to the text as read to you by your visitors. Follow along in your books. Note down any differences from the way you interpreted the text when you made your own markings. Evaluate the effectiveness of those differences. If you are unsure as to why another group made the decisions they did, ask the visitor.

Step Up and Present

Marking up the text in this way is meant as an exercise to point out the value of voice colour. Your goal is to develop an instinct for voice colour and do it naturally. Planning ahead of time as you did with the World Health Organization text can result in an artificial tone. On the other hand, if your group members give you a critique that recommends a wider range of voice colour, you might want to consciously annotate your text using the highlighting method above. That will point out to you places in the text where you can add some variety to your delivery to create interest and emphasis. After a while, it will become second nature.

Clarity

A variety of voice colour depends on vocal clarity in the first place. Your audience needs to be able to understand what you're saying without expending any effort. Don't require your audience to work very much in taking in what you are saying. You can never be sure how willing any group of people is to concentrate on your words. It is rather your responsibility to make your delivery as clear a possible. That is not to say that you cannot give an effective presentation unless you speak flawless English. Accents, for example, can make some deliveries interesting. The only time an accent is a problem is when it gets in the way of clarity. Sometimes clarity has to do with the way you use words and phrases. At other times it has to do with the way you enunciate them.

TASK TWO   Usage and Clarity

Listen to person 4 who will read two short presentations to you. That person will ask you a question after each presentation to test how clearly the message was delivered. Do not follow along in your text. Just listen as carefully as you can.

Person 4:   Read each of the following cases including title and text. When you are done, ask your group members the question that follows. After you hear the answers discuss with them any misunderstandings that came up and the possible reasons for them. A clarification of the original is below the question. Explain that clarification to the group after it has answered the question.

Case One

Presentation of Publishers at a Teachers' Staff Meeting

Thomson Publishing is really excited to present this new textbook to you. We think that you will find it a valuable resource for your courses. It is a new concept in pedagogy. It has many Canadian readings in it, but it is still a 4-in-1.

Question: *What did the presenter mean by the last sentence?*
Clarification: *Publishers uses the term "4-in-1" to refer to a textbook that has four parts or components in one text. Thus, the four means a rhetoric, a handbook, a reader, and research guide all in one book. The listener, however, might not hear "4-in-1," but rather "foreign one." That is even more likely when it is prefaced with references to Canadian readings. In this case, not only does the original feature of the text not get through, but the listeners might also begin to form opinions about using the text on erroneous information.*

Case Two

Telephone Conversation to an Employer about a Job Candidate

Yes, I have known him for several years. He worked in our shipping department first and later was in our accounting office. I did not know that he was looking for work in a completely different field. He was very popular with the other employees. What do I think of him? I can tell you that I can't recommend him too highly.

Question: What message did the reference give to you about the candidate?

Clarification: English allows for certain phrases that can have contradictory meanings. "I can't recommend him too highly" could mean that I cannot give him a high recommendation, or it could also mean that no matter how much praise I give him, it wouldn't be high enough. Phrases like "you can't imagine what kind of job he did" depend entirely on intonation to carry meaning. In this case, the listener might hear a completely opposite message from what was intended.

Enunciation and Clarity

TASK THREE

Part One

Work in pairs for this task. One person of the pair reads out the following list once in random order. The other person writes down the numbers of the words heard in the table below. When done, compare the order to see how clearly the words and phrases were enunciated. When you are finished, switch roles.

1. Bad bet
2. Perfect presence
3. She should say "sticks"
4. Bad bed
5. Sit by the rink
6. Perfect presents
7. Boat's swell
8. Stocking boxes
9. She should say "sixths"
10. Sit by the ring
11. Stacking boxes
12. Bodes well

Order in which the words and phrases were read:

Part Two

Read the following tongue twisters to each other. Determine which ones give your partner the most trouble. Isolate the particular sounds in those words that he or she needs to work on.

Which wristwatches are Swiss wristwatches?

Mrs. Smith's Fish Sauce shop

Three free throws

Six sticky sucker sticks

Hi-tech traveling tractor trailer truck tracker

Six sick slick slim sycamore saplings

Pope Sixtus VI's six texts

Which witch wished which wicked wish?

Your partner in Parts One and Two of this task will give you feedback on how well you enunciate. If you discover that your listeners sometimes miss some of yours words, pay special attention to those particular sounds as they come up in your presentations.

◁

In Summary

Take three minutes to write a summary of what you learned from participating in the tasks of Unit 9.

UNIT 10
Using Your Body

Here's what you'll work on in this unit.

- Determining the impact of physical elements on a presentation
- Developing solutions for ineffective physical delivery
- Identifying key physical elements
- Determining strategies for movement and gesture
- Marking a text for physical delivery

Effective delivery depends on more than your voice quality. What you do with your body also has a powerful impact on the success of your presentation. The following article is a good example of just how important attention to the physical elements of your presentation is.

The Kennedy-Nixon Presidential Debates, 1960

On 26 September 1960, 70 million U.S. viewers tuned in to watch Senator John Kennedy of Massachusetts and Vice President Richard Nixon in the first-ever televised presidential debate. It was the first of four televised "Great Debates" between Kennedy and Nixon. The first debate centered on domestic issues. The high point of the second debate, on 7 October, was disagreement over U.S. involvement in two small islands off the coast of China, and on 13 October, Nixon and Kennedy continued this dispute. On 21 October, the final debate, the candidates focused on American relations with Cuba.

The Great Debates marked television's grand entrance into presidential politics. They afforded the first real opportunity for voters to see their candidates in competition, and the visual contrast was dramatic. In August, Nixon had seriously injured his knee and spent two weeks in the hospital. By the time of the first debate he was still twenty pounds underweight, his pallor still poor. He arrived at the debate in an ill-fitting shirt, and refused make-up to improve his color and lighten his perpetual "5 o'clock shadow." Kennedy, by contrast, had spent early September campaigning in California. He was tan and confident and well-rested. "I had never seen him looking so fit," Nixon later wrote.

In substance, the candidates were much more evenly matched. Indeed, those who heard the first debate on the radio pronounced Nixon the winner. But the 70 million who watched television saw a candidate still sickly and obviously discomforted by Kennedy's smooth delivery and charisma. Those television viewers focused on what they saw, not what they heard. Studies of the audience indicated that, among television viewers, Kennedy was perceived the winner of the first debate by a very large margin.

Erika Tyner Allen

Available at: http://www.museum.tv/archives/etv/K/htmlK/kennedy-nixon/kennedy-nixon.htm

Appearance

The Kennedy-Nixon presidential debates in 1960 show that aside from movement and gesture, appearance can have a strong impact on the effectiveness of a presentation as well. You worked on the rhetorical triangle as an audience analysis tool in an earlier unit. That tool helped you to determine the audience's needs and to work out an approach you will use in giving your presentation. Part of that approach involves dress and appearance in general. Dressing formally would not enhance your message for some audiences, while it would be essential for others. Even if the presentation is casual, consider what messages clothing might be sending. If a presenter wears a T-shirt with a slogan or message not connected to the talk, he or she risks losing the audience as it reads and thinks about it. If the listener dislikes the message on the T-shirt, receptivity of your presentation message might be affected even though it is entirely unrelated.

TASK ONE   Dressing the Part

Work on this task individually. Compile a list of do's and don'ts for dress when giving a presentation. Your resources for this task are your experience, public speaking Web sites, and texts. Use the form on page 105. Bring the completed form to the next class session and exchange it with other group members. Write your comments on your group members' lists in the Reader's Comments column.

DO'S AND DON'TS FOR DRESSING FOR A PRESENTATION

Do	Don't	Reader's Comments

Impact of Physical Delivery on a Presentation

Even if a speaker's presentation is enhanced with good oral skills, it may suffer from lack of attention to physical skills. You will examine some of these skills in this unit and work out a set of strategies for your own upcoming presentations.

Part One

Each person is this exercise has a separate task. Read only your task and take 10 minutes to prepare a presentation to give to your group. You will give the presentation in Part Two of this task.

Person 1: Give a two to three minute presentation to the group on any subject that you know very well. The subject might be an interest, a class you recently attended, a strong opinion you have, or even just a plot summary of a book or movie. The point of this presentation is not the content, but rather how you give it. While you give the presentation, keep both hands in your pockets at all times. One hand should occasionally jiggle coins or keys. Stand with slumped shoulders and look at the ground. Never look at the group. Keep your face completely without expression. Do not move your feet.

Person 2: Give a two to three minute presentation to the group on any subject that you know very well. The subject might be an interest, a class you recently attended, a strong opinion you have, or even just a plot summary of a book or movie. The point of this presentation is not the content, but rather how you give it. While you give the presentation, adjust your hair and clothing repeatedly. Shift back and forth constantly from one foot to the other.

Person 3: Give a two to three minute presentation to the group on any subject that you know very well. The subject might be an interest, a class you recently attended, a strong opinion you have, or even just a plot summary of a book or movie. The point of this presentation is not the content, but rather how you give it. While you give the presentation, lean over a desk or a chair. Frown and look as bored as you can. Fidget with a pen in one hand. Scratch your head or face on occasion.

Person 4: Give a two to three minute presentation to the group on any subject that you know very well. The subject might be an interest, a class you recently attended, a strong opinion you have, or even just a plot summary of a book or movie. The point of this presentation is not the content, but rather how you give it. Never stop gesturing. Keep your hands constantly going describing what you are saying, pointing to your audience and emphasizing points. At the same time, keep moving your body. Step forward, side-to-side, and to the back without stopping.

Part Two

Each person gives the presentation in order of number. When finished, the presenter asks the group to

Step Up and Present

- name the physical components of the delivery,
- identify their impact on the effectiveness of the presentation, and

- make suggestions as to what the speaker should do to improve the physical delivery of the presentation.

Write the responses using the forms provided. Name the specific physical components of the presentation in the column entitled Physical Components. Identify the impact that that physical component had on the overall effectiveness of the presentation in the column entitled Effect. Finally, record suggestions for a more effective delivery under Solution.

PERSON 1

Topic		
Physical Component	**Effect**	**Solution**

PERSON 2

Topic		
Physical Component	**Effect**	**Solution**

PERSON 3

Topic		
Physical Component	**Effect**	**Solution**

PERSON 4

Topic		
Physical Component	**Effect**	**Solution**

◁

Focus and Emphasis

Physical delivery, like oral delivery, has a wide range of options. Just as voice colour helps create interest, a variety of movement and gesture helps keep the audience focused. A person who rarely moves or gestures is difficult to look at for very long. When the audience stops looking, it might also stop listening. Too much movement, on the other hand, can make the speaker look excessively nervous. At the very least, it will distract the listener from taking in the entire message. The ideal is clear, directed movement that works closely with voice colour in effective ways to emphasize points. Vigorous vocal delivery at a high rate and volume are often linked with animated gesture. The important thing is that gesture and movement, just like voice colour, must grow naturally out of your relationship with the text.

Identifying the Physical Elements   TASK THREE

Part One

This task asks you to consider when you would use physical elements in a presentation. The group will consider a number of these elements in turn, and discuss when and how to use them.

Person 3: Read out the physical element.

Person 2: Facilitate the group discussion.

Person 1: Record the group's responses in the table below.

Person 4: Keep time for this activity. The group has 15 minutes. Keep the group aware as to how much time remains.

Physical Component	When It Would Be Appropriate	What Should Be Done And/Or Avoided At the Same Time
Walking freely about the presentation area		
Walking about, but regularly returning to the lectern		
Never leaving the lectern		
Animated facial expression including big smiles, frowns, and intense looks		
Pointing directly at the listeners		
Large gestures with both hands		
Small gestures with both hands		
Little or no gesture		

Marking the Text

If your group gives you a critique that includes suggestions for more movement and gesture, you may want to use an annotated text much in the same way you did when you planned voice colour. Just as with voice colour, planned movement and gesture can look stilted and artificial. It is still a useful exercise in a class like this one, however, because you will get the hang of it during exercises and presentations. Eventually, physical delivery, too, becomes second nature.

TASK FOUR Providing Directions

In this task, you will help to provide directions that will assist a presenter deliver a text with clear, directed movement and gesture. Use the text you worked on for voice colour to work out what the physical delivery should be. When would you move about? When and how would you gesture? What should be happening with facial expression? Use the components identified in the chart above and add any more that you think the text requires. Use arrows or any other symbols that work for you.

Part One

Person 3: Run a group discussion on specific suggestions regarding physical delivery for the text.

Person 2: Annotate the text below according to the suggestions of the group.

We know from the World Health Organization that over three million children in developing countries die each year from being underweight. In developed countries, obesity is one of the leading causes of death. More than one-third of all disease in those countries results from overweight, which causes high blood pressure and high cholesterol levels. Alcohol and tobacco use compound the problem. These contribute to the primary killer in developed countries, cardio-vascular disease. While people in developing countries die from malnutrition, more than 4 million people die each year in developed countries from high cholesterol, almost 5 million from to tobacco use, and an incredible 7 million die from high blood pressure. What can we do about this? What can you do about this? First, start with yourself. Pay attention to your diet and stress factors. Check your blood pressure regularly. Get into good exercise and diet habits. Second, develop a global awareness. Respond generously to appeals for food aid to developing countries. Third, consider contributing your time to an organization that helps these people or even volunteer to work in developing countries to make life better for others who have so little.

Part Two

Person 2: Deliver the presentation to your group using the annotated text.

Persons 1, 3, and 4: Make suggestions to person 2 to improve the physical delivery of the text.

Step Up and Present

In Summary

Take three minutes to write a summary of what you learned from participating in the tasks of Unit 10.

UNIT 11

Using Visuals

Here's what you'll work on in this unit.

- Listing the advantages of using visuals in a presentation
- Developing strategies for using use three-dimensional visuals
- Determining design principles for two-dimensional visuals
- Examining principles for using presentation software
- Analyzing the reasons for caution when using visuals

So far, you have considered what your audience needs and how to meet those needs through vocal colour and the physical delivery of your message. Another component of presentations is the visual. A visual can be anything from a poster to a PowerPoint slide. Effective presenters know not only when but also how to use visuals well. This unit will ask you to consider visuals, develop some strategies for their use, and try them out for yourself.

Why Should You Use Visuals?

Not every presentation you attend will use visuals. Some presentations just don't require them. It is not a good idea to labour over trying to find some opportunity to use a visual when it just wouldn't be useful. On the other hand, it is a good idea to consider whether or not a visual would enhance what you are saying. Imagine yourself as a member of the audience. Would a visual make the presentation clearer, more interesting, and, perhaps, more persuasive? If so, exactly what kind of visual would be helpful as opposed to gratuitous or even distracting?

TASK ONE   Identifying the Advantages of Visuals

From the presenter's point of view, planning a visual can have many advantages. The following cases illustrate some of them.

Person 2: Read each of the following cases to the group.

Person 3: Facilitate a brief discussion after each case. The group's task is to identify the specific advantages the presenter enjoyed when using the visual. When the group has finished discussing all three cases, ask if anyone can add any additional advantages to the list.

Person 4: Record the advantages in the table following the cases.

Person 1: Be prepared to report the advantages to the class when called upon.

Case One

A student gives a first presentation in a speaking class. She is speaking about her interest in snorkelling. The student is well-prepared, but nervous. She knows she should maintain good eye contact, but finds it difficult to keep looking at everyone. Despite having planned some gestures, she hears during a critique session that they appeared a little awkward and needed more coordination with the content of her talk. She was advised to try using a visual.

Part Two of the assignment asks her to give the presentation again and incorporate the suggestions she received from the critique. She gives the presentation, but this time brings in a snorkel. When she indicates the snorkel, both she and the audience look at it. Holding the snorkel and referring to its parts gives her numerous opportunities for natural gesture. Finally, she discovers that she does not need to glance at her notes as much as the first time, because the parts of the snorkel themselves remind her of what she needs to talk about next.

Case Two

An architect explains to a client the advantages of using a radiant flooring system. He spends 15 minutes explaining the system so that he can outline the reasons why the client should accept his recommendation to use it in the building's design. The client begins to ask a number of questions requiring the architect to go over the same ground several times. In the end, the client leaves saying he will think about it.

The next time the architect explains radiant flooring systems to a client, he brings out a colour coded drawing. As he explains it to the customer, he points to the various components. He finds he has used half the time and the client grasps the advantages of the system at once.

Case Three

A psychologist is presenting a talk to a group of high school students on the effect of watching television and surfing the internet on academic success. She can see as she delivers her talk that many of them have tuned out. Those who are listening look skeptical. The talk ends with only one or two questions from the floor.

She changes her presentation for the next school she visits. This time, she uses large projected graphs from a large Canadian study that shows a clear relationship between a great deal of television watching and low attention span. Another graph shows a dramatic relationship between time surfing the internet and failure rates. This time, everyone is tuned in and focused on her visuals. She gets many questions, which spark a lively discussion.

ADVANTAGES OF USING VISUALS

1.	
2.	
3.	
4.	
5.	
6.	
7.	
8.	
9.	
10.	
11.	
12.	

Now that you have identified the advantages of using visuals in your presentations, consider how you will actually use them. One way of thinking of the visuals available to you is to categorize them into two types: three dimensional and two dimensional. Each of them needs to be handled in a way that keeps the need of the audience in focus.

The Three-Dimensional Visual

Part One

Person 3: Read the following directions to your group.

Each person has ten minutes to locate an object somewhere in the room and devise a two to three minute presentation that prominently uses the object. The presentation can instruct the listeners how to use the object, sell the object, compare and contrast it to something else, or just about anything the presenter wants to do as long as the object is used.

Part Two

The group gives the presentations in order of number. Each person in the group fills in the following feedback form after each presenter.

Step Up and Present

FEEDBACK FORM

Presenter Number	What Worked Well When Using the Visual	Suggestions for Improvement When Using the Visual
Presenter 1		
Presenter 2		
Presenter 3		
Presenter 4		

Part Three

Person 2: Manage a group critique session. Ask each person to present the feedback on each presenter in turn. Point out any agreement the group has as to how a three-dimensional visual should be used.

Person 1: Record the consensus on how to use a three-dimensional visual in the checklist form below.

Person 4: Be prepared to report the findings to the class.

WHEN USING A THREE-DIMENSIONAL VISUAL, THE PRESENTER SHOULD

✔ _____

✔ _____

✔ _____

✔ _____

✔ _____

✔ _____

✔ _____

✔ _____

✔ _____

◁

The Two-Dimensional Visual

Two-dimensional visuals are commonly used in presentations. These visuals can include bar charts, graphs, photographs, and projected computer programs like PowerPoint. Some presentation rooms are equipped with document cameras that allow you to project a small visual onto a large screen. Others have overhead projectors which require you to transfer your visual to a transparency first. Yet, other rooms do not have any facilities for you to use requiring you to bring in large visuals on boards or posters. As you discovered above, visuals can make your message clearer and more effective. On the other hand, they can also overwhelm the audience, distract it from your main points, and confuse it if not handled well. The following task asks you to examine some visuals used in presentations and decide how they could be improved.

Part One

Person 3:   Read out the following directions to the group.

Everyone leaves your group for this task. All the number 1s from all groups form a new group as do the 2s, 3s, and 4s. When you have arrived in your new group, appoint a facilitator who will keep the discussion moving and a timekeeper who will keep the group posted as to how much time is left. The groups have 20 minutes to complete the task. The goal of this task is to analyze the visual assigned to your group and develop a five-minute analysis and lesson around it. What works well in the visual? What doesn't work well? Why? How can it be improved? What general principles about preparing a visual can be derived from this analysis? When 20 minutes has passed, each person will be asked to return to the original group to present the lesson.

Visual for Group 1

Appropriate Visuals for Presentations

For years, research has shown that people retain more of what they hear when they see and hear the information at the same time. Good presenters have always understood the importance of <u>appropriate</u> visuals in getting their message across. Now with the advent of electronic presentation tools such as *Microsoft PowerPoint* or *Corel Presentations*, we have the ability to easily produce a relatively sophisticated visual presentation.

When used <u>properly</u>, visual aids can effectively enhance the presentation. People remember 40 percent more when they hear and see something simultaneously. Many people today use presentation software, such as *Microsoft PowerPoint* or *Corel Presentations*, to present visuals. Either of these software programs is easy to use and extremely effective.

Your presentation materials are displayed to the audience on a computer screen or a projection system. Unless your audience is <u>very small</u> (three or four people who can gather around a computer), you should use a large projection screen. You can also establish links to Websites within your presentation.

For example, assume you are doing a presentation on Chinese culture. You can use a Web link to show some of the historical sites in China. You can also use the presentation program to establish a virtual seminar by placing a number of Presentations or PowerPoint presentations from various presenters on the Web.

HIV/AIDS has had, and continues to have, substantial and sometimes dramatic impacts on mortality levels in countries most seriously affected. However, AIDS will not overcome the momentum of population growth at the regional level, even in Sub-Saharan Africa. This will be true particularly if changes in behavior, already observed in some settings, bring about an early curtailment of HIV infections in affected countries.

2000	6,079,603,571	1.21	74,198
2001	6,153,801,961	1.18	73,131
2002	6,226,933,918	1.16	72,829
2003	6,299,763,405	1.15	73,034
2004	6,372,797,742	1.14	73,333
2005	6,446,131,400	1.13	73,513
2006	6,519,645,083	1.12	73,671
2007	6,593,316,984	1.12	73,955
2008	6,667,272,341	1.11	74,218
2009	6,741,491,221	1.10	74,400
2010	6,815,892,190	1.09	74,590
2011	6,890,482,439	1.08	74,702
2012	6,965,184,730	1.06	74,506
2013	7,039,691,203	1.05	74,049
2014	7,113,740,413	1.03	73,343
2015	7,187,084,263	1.00	72,593
2016	7,259,678,024	0.99	71,875
2017	7,331,553,922	0.96	71,047
2018	7,402,601,692	0.94	70,110
2019	7,472,711,767	0.92	69,061

INCEASE IN THE NUMBER OF CASES IN CANADA

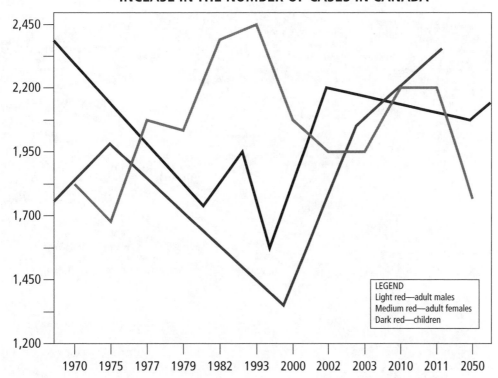

LEGEND
Light red—adult males
Medium red—adult females
Dark red—children

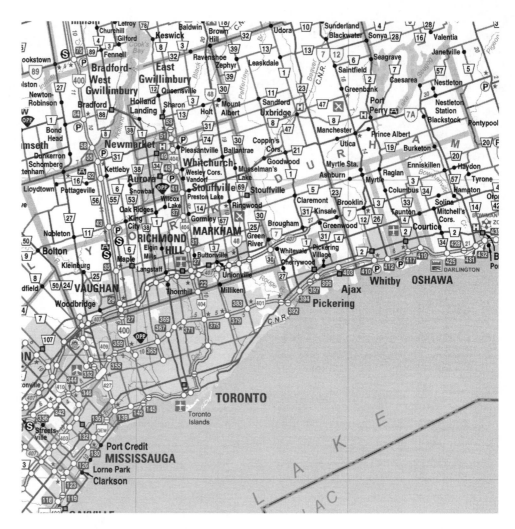

© Queen's Printer for Ontario, 2005. Reproduced with permission.

Part Two

Give your presentation in order of number after you have returned to your group. Record the main principles that come out of each presentation in the table below. Add any additional ideas as they occur to you.

PRINCIPLES OF EFFECTIVE VISUAL DESIGN

1.	
2.	
3.	
4.	
5.	
6.	
7.	
8.	
9.	
10.	
11.	
12.	
13.	
14.	
15.	

Using Presentation Software

Many presenters choose to enhance their presentations by using presentation software like PowerPoint to develop a slide show. Such an approach can provide many advantages. You will be able to provide colourful, memorable visuals that will make your ideas concrete. Small images and text can easily be magnified so that everyone gets a clear view. In addition, program options permit a lively presentation with subtitles that fly in from off screen, dissolves, sound effects, and animation. You can even add a short video clip.

This large range of choices requires some control over your material, otherwise the slide show can easily become distracting rather than helpful. Just because the program permits options, it is not necessary or even desirable to use all the available formats. Many beginner presenters make the mistake of thinking that every presentation needs to use such software. The danger here is that such slide shows can become an easy way out, requiring little creativity or originality. Audiences that have seen many such presentations can become impatient with them because they are so similar. The lights go out and the presenter is no longer the focal point. Slides continue throughout the presentation using templates that the audience has seen umpteen times before. The result is that the exact opposite of what was intended is achieved. Rather than providing a memorable experience that engages the audience in a tailored format, the presentation becomes generic, bland, and, to some extent, tiresome.

Hint

A general principle when designing a computer generated slide show is to draw attention to the content rather than to the presentation method. Ask yourself what your motive is for each slide. Does the slide serve to clarify the content or is it there so that the audience will admire the visual?

If you choose to use this technology, keep a few things in mind.

- A presentation is not better just because it uses slides. Consider all your options rather than automatically selecting this technology.
- Size up your presentation situation. Does it have all the equipment and software that you would require? Are the sight lines good for everyone in the room?
- Make sure you test out the equipment and run your file on it before the presentation date to be sure you won't have any problems. Be sure to make and bring backup copies of your presentation.
- Avoid running slides all the way through your presentation. Provide an introduction first. Use slides only when appropriate. Mute the projection between sections or at least provide some background image between slides.
- Keep each slide simple. Avoid putting up too much text or complicated images that will entirely draw the attention of the audience away from you so that they can read the slide or figure out the image.
- Avoid using common templates. If you have decided to use the program, design your own distinctive formats and backgrounds.
- Plan what you will do if the equipment or program fails. Have a backup plan so that you are not totally dependent on the technology to complete your presentation.

A Few Cautions

Using a visual can improve a presentation if you keep a few cautions in mind. Each speaking situation is unique and you will need to adapt to the audience and to the facilities available to you.

Determining Cautions

Person 4: Facilitate the discussion of each of the following cautions. The group's task is to determine what a presenter needs to be careful about in each one. Ask everyone to write the reason for the caution in the space provided below each item after the group has come to its conclusion.

Caution 1

Teachers have traditionally used chalkboards or whiteboards as they work with a class. Be careful, however, about using these tools because they have a major disadvantage.

WHAT IS THAT DISADVANTAGE?

_____

_____

_____

_____

Caution 2

You might have pamphlets, sheets of paper, or objects to pass around. It can be very problematic to pass these out at the beginning or during a presentation. If you have them, it is usually best to give them to your audience just as you finish.

WHY IS THAT BETTER THAN HANDING THEM OUT DURING THE PRESENTATION?

_____

_____

_____

_____

Caution 3

Visuals should not require set-up time during the presentation. Be sure that you can use them and dispense with them quickly. Avoid any long periods of silence while you are working with your visual.

WHY IS ELIMINATING SET-UP TIME AND PERIODS OF SILENCE SO IMPORTANT?

_____

_____

_____

_____

Caution 4

Avoid using too many visuals either of the same kind or of different kinds. Select just a few appropriate and highly effective visuals to make your point rather than presenting a lot of visual stimuli to your audience.

WHAT IS THE PROBLEM WITH TOO MANY VISUALS?

_____

_____

_____

_____

In Summary

Take three minutes to write a summary of what you learned from participating in the tasks of Unit II.

_____

_____

_____

_____

_____

Part 3

Applications

The first two parts of this book asked you to work through a number of tasks around preparing and delivering a presentation. Part 3 will ask you to apply what you have learned to specific speaking situations. First, you will have specific expository presentation problems to solve. You will then go a step further and deliver persuasive talks. In addition to giving full, individual formal presentations, you will also work through the process of preparing and delivering a group presentation in Unit 14. Finally, you will try out different strategies for speaking at meetings.

UNIT 12

Expository Presentations

Here's what you'll work on in this unit.

- Developing a presentation outline
- Preparing and delivering a personal expository presentation
- Preparing and delivering an informative expository presentation
- Preparing and delivering an instructive expository presentation
- Critiquing expository presentations

An expository presentation explains something new to the listener. The presenter wants the audience to understand rather than to agree or take action. That means the presentation is more objective than subjective. You will give expository presentations in this unit. Naturally, you will have your point of view and preferences that in some way will come through the presentation. The choices you make as to what information to use and how to organize it begin to convey your perspective on the subject. As far as possible, however, keep expository presentations balanced. Give both sides of an issue, outline the advantages as well as the disadvantages of the topic, and present the various facets of your subject that will help the listener comprehend.

You likely have already given expository presentations in a classroom. These assignments ask you to find out something you did not know before and make it understandable to your classmates. A project like this involves a number of challenges.

First, you have to decide the scope of your research and just what your resources will be. Second, you need to evaluate the information and select what would be helpful to your audience as opposed to what might be unnecessary or even confusing at this point.

Third, you need to tailor your data by organizing it in a way that connects with the audience. The process is very similar to writing a research paper, but in this case you are organizing to be heard rather than to be read. That means you need to think about

- visual support,
- emphasis through repetition and summary, and
- ways to interact with your listener through techniques like questioning.

Many people find that they continue to give expository presentations in their workplaces. You might be sent to a seminar or conference, for example, and asked to brief your colleagues when you return. You might have to give a progress report or present the background to a company project. Another kind of expository presentation is instructive. You might be asked to train new hires or teach clients how to operate equipment. In all these cases, your main goal is to make the unfamiliar familiar.

Organizing

When you are ready to put an expository presentation together, consider how you will organize it. In some cases, the organization is obvious. It flows naturally out of what you are doing. If you are instructing, for example, the best approach is sequential. You teach what to do first. The second builds on the first, the third builds on the second and so on. If you are describing a subject, a building for example, you will start at one point and then move from part to part. Consequently, you could begin with the foundation and move up to the roof. Other subjects do not readily offer you an organizational pattern. In that case, take a look at the information you have collected. Match it to your audience analysis using the rhetorical triangle. Decide what information best suits what you determined the audience need is. You can take out anything that you deem to be too technical or confusing at this stage. Put together a point form outline that includes notes as to what kind of visual support or interactive strategies you might use.

Here is an example.

Sample Case

A municipality is sponsoring a multi-cultural festival. One of the highlights is the performance of the local Peking Opera company. The presenter's task is to help prepare the small audience in a studio space for what it is about to see. He has 45 minutes before the short opera begins. After some research, the presenter developed the following outline.

1.0 Introduction	Ask how many people in the audience have ever seen a Chinese opera. Ask for impressions.
	My connection with the Chinese theatre.
	Purpose: to prepare the audience for what they are about to see.
2.0 Differences between Western stages and Chinese stages	
2.1 Location:	Traditional Chinese theatres were primarily outdoor and located in market places or in front of temples in contrast with the indoor theatre structure of the West.
2.2 Design:	Open on three sides, no scenery, no special lighting in contrast with the traditional Western proscenium stage with scenery and lighting facilities.

Musicians on the stage in full view of the audience.

Visual (slide)

- show a slide of a stage
- point out main features
- gesture to the set-up of the performance space around which the audience is gathered
- go over to the musicians

3.0 Differences between Western acting and Chinese acting

3.1 Role types:

Chinese actors specialize their whole lives in one of four major role types as opposed to Western characters who work on a broader range. Each type has particular vocal and physical technique as well as distinctive costume and make-up.

Audio/Visual (slides and tape)

- female—show slide—play tape of voice
- male—show slide—play tape of voice
- clown—show slide—play tape of voice
- painted face—show slide—play tape of voice

3.2 Performance technique:

Chinese theatre uses mime and symbolic props in contrast to the general realism of Western theatre.

Visuals (props)

- show a horse whip used to represent a horse
- show how to ride a horse a great distance
- show how to open a door and enter a room

4.0 Differences between Western plays and Chinese plays

4.1 Use of music:

Mixture of speech, song, and poetry as opposed to spoken, natural speech throughout in most Western dramas—compare to a Western musical.

4.2 Sources of stories:	Chinese traditional plays are based on famous novels, legends, and history as opposed to the Western approach of new pieces by playwrights every year on contemporary themes.
	Summary of the short play the audience will see.
5.0 Conclusion	Restate the main elements the audience is about to see. Wish them an enjoyable show. Open the floor to questions until the end of the presentation.

Analysis

This presenter chose to leave out all the history connected with Peking Opera in order to focus on those elements that the audience was about to see. He used both visual and audio examples to help prepare the audience for a very different experience. Finally, he built in a question period to address any audience concerns.

The Personal Presentation

Some subjects are close to you. They are a part of your life and help define who you are. These presentations may require some research, but you generally know a great deal already. The key for an effective personal presentation is to let your passion for the subject come through. That will give your presentation authenticity. The audience will see that this subject really matters to the speaker. In this way, your presentation becomes more interesting. At the same time, keep in mind that you are the expert here. The audience may have only a passing familiarity with your subject. Your listener needs you to select just the right amount of information and relate it to what is already familiar.

Personal Expository Presentation   **TASK ONE**

Part One

Person 2:   Read the following instructions to the group and facilitate the activity.

Each member of the group will prepare an individual personal presentation. Your task is to choose some aspect of your background that you think members of your group are unfamiliar with. You might select an interest, an involvement in some activity, an aspect of your cultural background, or just about anything that you are interested in and are willing to share. Take 20 minutes and prepare a preliminary outline that indicates the aspects your talk will cover, what visuals you would need, and any specific techniques you wish to employ for your opening and closing.

Hint

Choose a subject with which you are already very familiar and do not need to research. You can use the outline model provided earlier in the unit. A blank rhetorical triangle and outline form follow this task. Use them to prepare your talk. Remember to leave the assessor's column blank.

Person 4: Keep time for this activity and remind the group when time is close to running out.

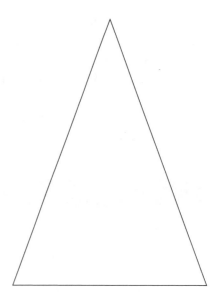

OUTLINE FORM

Unit	Audio/Visual	Assessor's Comments/Questions
Introduction		
Body		
Conclusion		

Part Two

Person 2: Coordinate the following activity. Ask the group members to exchange their proposed outlines and then make comments in the assessor's column. When the timekeeper signals the first 10 minutes, ask everyone to exchange with yet another person and add further comments. Finally, return the proposal to the writer.

Person 1: Keep track of the time. Warn the group when each of the 10-minute periods is about to end.

You now have a preliminary outline along with feedback from two group members. Take your proposed outline, look at the comments, and rework your plans for your presentation. Prepare whatever visuals you might need and be ready to give your presentation next session.

Step Up and Present

Present your personal expository presentation to your group. In addition, critique the presentations of the other members of your group. Use the Presentation Critique Forms as you watch the presentation. Give the completed critique sheet to the presenter after the presentation is done.

Hint

You will need one critique form for each presenter. Reproduce the form on page 135 so you have as many as you need. Check off the appropriate boxes and indicate specific examples of what you mean by your comment in the For Example column. Write specific suggestions and comments at the bottom.

Part Three

Read the assessments you received from your group members. Look over your outline and evaluate your presentation. Did it accomplish what you wanted it to? Was there anything you should have done differently? Imagine that you were asked to give the same presentation again. Would you make any changes? Write a brief self-assessment using the spaces provided.

TOPIC:

PRESENTATION CRITIQUE FORM

Assessor's Name_____ For Presenter_____ Topic_____

Oral Delivery | | | | **For Example**
Volume | Just the right volume | ❏
| Needs more volume | ❏
| Needs less volume | ❏
| Generally appropriate except for | ❏

Voice Colour | Good variety of pitch and rate | ❏
| Needs a greater variety of pitch | ❏
| Needs more variety in rate | ❏
| Generally appropriate except for | ❏

Physical Delivery
Gesture and | Just the right use of natural gesture | ❏
Movement | Needs more gesture | ❏
| Strong, consistent eye contact | ❏
| Needs more eye contact with entire group | ❏
| Excessive movement was distracting | ❏
| Generally appropriate except for | ❏

Introduction
Hook | Effective | ❏
| Needs to be stronger | ❏
Background | Sufficient | ❏
| Needs more background | ❏
Thesis | Clear | ❏
| Needs a clearer thesis statement | ❏

Body
Points | Appropriate number | ❏
| Reduce the number of points | ❏
| Add more points | ❏
| Clear/well supported | ❏
| Provide more explanation | ❏

Visuals | Effective | ❏
| Reduce the number of visuals | ❏
| Add more visuals | ❏
| Visuals need to be clearer | ❏

Conclusion | Effective | ❏
| Included new points | ❏
| Abrupt | ❏
| Needs | ❏

Additional
Comments and
Suggestions:

WHAT I WOULD KEEP IF I DID THE PRESENTATION AGAIN:

_____

_____

_____

_____

WHAT I WOULD DO DIFFERENTLY IF I DID THE PRESENTATION AGAIN:

_____

_____

_____

_____

OVERALL, I WOULD SAY THAT MY PRESENTATION

_____

_____

_____

_____

The Informative Presentation

An informative presentation requires research. You might need to use libraries, retrieve material from electronic databases, or interview people to get what you need to accomplish the task. Be sure to establish your credibility during the talk by referring to your sources. If you have some important statistics, let your audience know where you got them. Your job is not to convince the audience that one position or another is the right one. In fact, the audience should not be able to really tell what side you are on. Thus, specific information and equal treatment to different sides of the issue are key to accomplishing your task.

Hints

- Be sure to avoid confusing the audience with too much information.
- Establish the credibility of your material by referring to your sources.
- Give a fair statement of the different positions.
- Resist expressing an opinion in this type of presentation.

Part One

Person 2:   Read the following instructions to the group.

Select a regional or national issue upon which people disagree. Your task is to find out the necessary background and the reasons behind the differing viewpoints. Prepare an eight- to ten-minute presentation suitable for a community center in your neighbourhood. You can use the blank rhetorical triangle and outline form below to prepare your presentation. List your research sources for this presentation in the space provided. Ask one of your group members to fill out the assessor's comments and questions column when you have finished the proposed outline. Rework the outline if necessary.

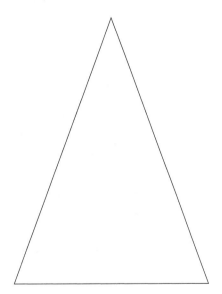

OUTLINE FORM

Unit	Audio/Visual	Assessor's Comments/Questions
Introduction		
Body		
Conclusion		

Research Sources for the Informative Expository Presentation

Part Two

Present your informative expository presentation. In addition, critique the presentations of the other members of your group.

Step Up and Present

Hint

You will need one critique form for each presenter. Reproduce the form on page 140 so you have as many as you need. Check off the appropriate boxes and indicate specific examples of what you mean by your comment in the For Example column. Write specific suggestions and comments at the bottom.

PRESENTATION CRITIQUE FORM

Assessor's Name_____ For Presenter_____ Topic_____

				For Example
Oral Delivery				
Volume	Just the right volume	❏		
	Needs more volume	❏		
	Needs less volume	❏		
	Generally appropriate except for	❏		
Voice Colour	Good variety of pitch and rate	❏		
	Needs a greater variety of pitch	❏		
	Needs more variety in rate	❏		
	Generally appropriate except for	❏		
Physical Delivery				
Gesture and Movement	Just the right use of natural gesture	❏		
	Needs more gesture	❏		
	Strong, consistent eye contact	❏		
	Needs more eye contact with entire group	❏		
	Excessive movement was distracting	❏		
	Generally appropriate except for	❏		
Introduction				
Hook	Effective	❏		
	Needs to be stronger	❏		
Background	Sufficient	❏		
	Needs more background	❏		
Thesis	Clear	❏		
	Needs a clearer thesis statement	❏		
Body				
Points	Appropriate number	❏		
	Clear reference to sources	❏		
	Need to indicate sources	❏		
	Credibility well established	❏		
	Credibility needs to be established	❏		
	Different positions evenly presented	❏		
	Needs a fuller treatment of different views	❏		
	Clear/well supported	❏		
	Provide more explanation	❏		
Visuals	Effective	❏		
	Reduce the number of visuals	❏		
	Add more visuals	❏		
	Visuals need to be clearer	❏		
Conclusion	Effective	❏		
	Included new points	❏		
	Abrupt	❏		
	Needs	❏		
Additional Comments and Suggestions:				

Part Three

Read the assessments you received from your group members. Look over your outline and evaluate your presentation. Did it accomplish what you wanted it to? Was there anything you should have done differently? Imagine that you were asked to give the same presentation again. Would you make any changes? Write a brief self-assessment using the spaces provided.

TOPIC:

_____

_____

_____

_____

WHAT I WOULD KEEP IF I DID THE PRESENTATION AGAIN:

_____

_____

_____

_____

WHAT I WOULD DO DIFFERENTLY IF I DID THE PRESENTATION AGAIN:

_____

_____

_____

_____

OVERALL, I WOULD SAY THAT MY PRESENTATION

_____

_____

_____

_____

The Instructive Presentation

Your goal in the last two presentations was for your audience to comprehend something it did not know much about before. When you instruct, you want the audience to move one step beyond comprehending. You want them to be able to do something. That means that you want them to be able to reproduce some skill or series of actions that produces a particular result. A teaching chef wants the students in the cooking class to make a successful soufflé. A restaurant manager wants the part-time cashier to use the cash register without error.

Organizing an instructive presentation means you need to break down the instructions into a series of tasks in order. It also requires you to think ahead. What possible mistakes could happen? What should the learner pay special attention to? What could be misunderstood? What materials or tools need to be prepared ahead of time? Finally, how will the learner know that he or she has done it right? What is the standard for comparison?

Hints

- Be sure to give sufficient background to the audience.
- Hold out a clear example of what the result should be.
- Identify up front all the tools and materials the learner will need.
- Provide warnings, cautions, or special notes before each step.
- Demonstrate as you instruct by using the materials and tools or other visuals.

TASK THREE   Instructive Expository Presentation

Part One

Person 4:   Read the following instructions to the group.

Develop an eight- to ten-minute presentation that teaches your classmates how to do something that you know how to do but which you judge most of them do not. Your goal is that after seeing your presentation they could state the materials and tools needed, describe the steps, explain the warnings and cautions, and do the procedure under some supervision. Use the blank rhetorical triangle and the outline form that follow. Ask one of your group members to fill out the Assessor's Comments/Questions column when you have finished the proposed outline. Look at the comments and rework the outline in any way necessary.

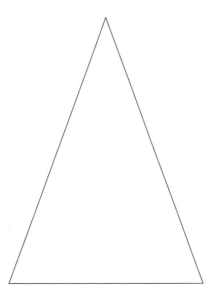

Materials and tools needed:

_____

_____

_____

_____

Steps in the procedure:

_____

_____

_____

_____

Warnings and cautions to highlight:

_____

_____

_____

_____

OUTLINE FORM

Unit	Audio/Visual	Assessor's Comments/Questions
Introduction		
Body		
Conclusion		

Part Two

Present your instructive expository presentation. In addition, critique the presentations of the other members of your group

Hint

You will need one critique form for each presenter. Reproduce the form on page 146 so you have as many as you need. Check off the appropriate boxes and indicate specific examples of what you mean by your comment in the For Example column. Write specific suggestions and comments at the bottom.

Part Three

Read the assessments you received from your group members. Look over your outline and evaluate your presentation. Did it accomplish what you wanted it to? Was there anything you should have done differently? Imagine that you were asked to give the same presentation again. Would you make any changes? Write a brief self-assessment in the spaces below and on page 147.

TOPIC:

WHAT I WOULD KEEP IF I DID THE PRESENTATION AGAIN:

PRESENTATION CRITIQUE FORM

Assessor's Name_____ For Presenter_____ Topic_____

Oral Delivery   **For Example**

Volume
Just the right volume ❏
Needs more volume ❏
Needs less volume ❏
Generally appropriate except for ❏

Voice Colour
Good variety of pitch and rate ❏
Needs a greater variety of pitch ❏
Needs more variety in rate ❏
Generally appropriate except for ❏

Physical Delivery

Gesture and
Movement
Just the right use of natural gesture ❏
Needs more gesture ❏
Strong, consistent eye contact ❏
Needs more eye contact with entire group ❏
Excessive movement was distracting ❏
Generally appropriate except for ❏

Introduction
Hook
Effective ❏
Needs to be stronger ❏
Background
Sufficient ❏
Needs more background ❏
Thesis
Clear ❏
Needs a clearer thesis statement ❏

Body
Points
Clear step-by-step instructions ❏
Some instructions need to be clearer ❏
Clear warnings and cautions ❏
Needs more warnings and cautions ❏
Materials and tools well identified ❏
Materials and tools need to be clearly identified ❏

Visuals
Effective ❏
Reduce the number of visuals ❏
Add more visuals ❏
Visuals need to be clearer ❏

Conclusion
Effective ❏
Included new points ❏
Abrupt ❏
Needs ❏

Additional
Comments and
Suggestions:

WHAT I WOULD DO DIFFERENTLY IF I DID THE PRESENTATION AGAIN:

_____

_____

_____

OVERALL, I WOULD SAY THAT MY PRESENTATION

_____

_____

_____

In Summary

Take three minutes to write a summary of what you learned from participating in the tasks of Unit 12.

_____

_____

_____

_____

_____

_____

_____

_____

_____

_____

_____

_____

_____

_____

_____

_____

_____

_____

_____

_____

UNIT 13

Persuasive Presentations

Here's what you'll work on in this unit.

- Determining specific goals and strategies for different persuasive presentations
- Outlining benefits in a persuasive presentation
- Developing an argument
- Refuting objections
- Preparing and delivering a persuasive presentation
- Preparing and delivering a marketing presentation
- Answering questions in an employment interview

You gave expository presentations because you wanted your listener to understand something new. The purpose was to make the unfamiliar familiar. The listener did not need to agree with or even like the subject. The emotional response and reasoned assent was not critical to what you were doing. What was critical was that you conveyed information in as objective a manner as possible. But there are times when you need to move beyond just conveying information or ideas. You need to get the listener onside. Your goal becomes to convince the audience that the particular position you have on your subject is the right one, and that it is in the best interest of the listener to accept it. You might be in a position where you are making a proposal at a board meeting, selling a product to a client, or presenting yourself to an employer as the best person for a job. All of these situations require you to convince the listener, possibly to change the listener's mind. In these cases, you cannot measure your success in the same way you did with expository presentations. In those cases, if your listener could restate the important points of your topic or reproduce a particular procedure, then you had succeeded. In a persuasive presentation, if the listener can correctly summarize your main points that is no indication that you have succeeded. The listener might understand you well, but believe that you have not really made a convincing case. If the board accepts your proposal, you have succeeded. If the client buys your product, you have succeeded. If the employer says, "you're hired," you have succeeded. Any other result means that your persuasive presentation did not work. That is why the persuasive presentation is the most difficult to get right. It requires

- thorough research both into the audience and into the subject,
- a clear statement of benefits,
- a strong case with irreproachable support, and
- an open and careful consideration of any objections.

Research

Audience

You have already used the rhetorical triangle several times for your presentations. It is a tool for you to first identify the experience your audience has with the subject and then to determine what it really needs from your presentation. The presentation should not waste time covering unnecessary ground or diverting the attention of your audience to something that would best suit a different one. Each listener has particular needs. Each audience has a profile that leads you to a common denominator with which you can work. For a persuasive presentation, this profile helps you in two main ways.

First, it helps you decide what kind of background information and support to choose. Does the audience already have some familiarity with the subject? Does the audience possibly have some misconceptions or connotations about the subject that need to be cleared up before you can start to convince it of anything? Is the audience possibly suspicious of you or what you represent? It is important to consider these questions before you put your presentation together. In an expository presentation, you gave information and ideas so that the audience could understand more. In a persuasive presentation, you will give information and ideas that clear the way for an argument and support the points of the argument as you go. If you don't clear the way before launching into your case, whatever you say might be filtered through some kind of misunderstanding in the mind of the listener.

Second, the profile helps you to determine both a reasonable object and a strategy to get there. You need to know if your audience is very much against or already inclined to your position or proposal at the beginning. That knowledge makes an enormous difference to what you can do. The following matrix summarizes what this could mean for your next persuasive presentation. Use it to decide what kind of audience you have in terms of your subject matter. Then, determine what you could reasonably accomplish with such an audience and the best means to do it.

PERSUASIVE PRESENTATION MATRIX

Type of Audience	Presentation Goal	Strategy
Hostile	It is unlikely that you can move a hostile audience to action or even agreement in a single presentation. In this case, your persuasive goal might just be that your audience accept that your position is reasonable and that some of your audience's objections are not as well founded as it might have thought. Thus, you will have moved the audience one step. Future presentations can take it further.	Since the audience is hostile to your position, it is likely to be suspicious of your evidence. It is important to use only immediately verifiable and reputable data. Give the sources of your information as you go. The presentation needs to emphasize reasoned argument rather than attempt to use an emotional appeal.
Disagree	An audience that simply disagrees rather than being hostile can be engaged on the issues. As with the hostile audience, it probably cannot be moved to action or enthusiasm about your point of view. On the other hand, you can move it away from disagreement. You can aim at making this audience open to accepting some of your points and to hearing more.	This audience needs you to do two things. You need to present your case clearly with well-documented support. You also need to clearly engage the reasons against your position one by one. The best approach is a relaxed, friendly, and open consideration of the case against you. Avoid any emotional appeal with this audience.
Neutral Because Unfamiliar	This audience has no preconceived ideas or misconceptions because the subject is very new to it. Thus, it does not hold any strong objections. Your presentation can first lead the audience to understanding the topic and then to agreeing with your viewpoint.	Your strategy needs to begin with an expository presentation and then shift to a persuasive one as you move on. You can begin with clear background, present supported reasons, declare your sources, and then use some emotional appeal.
Neutral Because Unconcerned	This audience knows something about the subject, but does not really care either way because the subject doesn't really concern it. The listener in this audience does not see a need to make any kind of decision around what you are talking about.	This audience needs a particular kind of background. The information, support, and examples that you present need to demonstrate that there is a connection between the topic and the audience. After you have demonstrated the listener's relationship to the subject, then interest the listener in your point of view. Highlight the reasonableness of your position and the benefits of agreeing with you.

Type of Audience	Presentation Goal	Strategy
Agreeable	If you know that your audience is generally agreeable to what you have to say, you can then move it to enthusiasm about your point of view. You can firm up agreement so that it is solid and thus prepare the listener to make a commitment later on.	Begin with the familiar and move to the unfamiliar. Reinforce the reasons why the audience is already in general agreement. You can use an emotional appeal here in addition to your supported points. Then, discuss objections to your point of view that the audience may have heard, and show it how to answer those objections and why they are not valid.
Enthusiastic	This audience is already on side with your ideas. It is ready to be moved to action. Your persuasive goal for this audience can be to get them to do something. That may be to publicly commit themselves, sign their names, or take some other step to further the subject of your presentation.	Since the audience is already on side, it does not need to be convinced. You don't need to provide as much documented information as with a neutral or negative audience. You can use an emotional appeal to lead or push your audience into taking a step forward. The presentation can end with an appeal to act and a clear description of the alternatives so that the audience knows exactly what it can do.

Evaluating the Target Audience   TASK ONE

Person 3: Facilitate this activity. Make sure everyone has a chance to speak.

Person 2: Keep time. Your group has 15 minutes to complete the activity.

Person 4: Record the results in the table below.

Person 1: Be prepared to share the results with the class after each part of the task.

Your team is a consulting group for presenters. Several have come to you with presentation projects looking for professional advice. Look at each of the following cases. Use the Persuasive Presentation Matrix above to determine what kind of audience the presenter is working with. Give specific advice to the presenter as to what he or she can reasonably expect to accomplish and how to go about it. Put your own opinions on the topics aside. Your purpose as a consultant is to give the best advice possible for the speaker to achieve success.

Case One

A residential neighbourhood has had considerable controversy lately. There is a proposal for a halfway house for convicted felons to be opened there. One of the few members of that community who is in support of the halfway house is going to present at a community meeting. She has come to you for advice.

Type of Audience	Goal for the Presentation	Strategy

Case Two

Coincidentally, the next day another member of that community comes to you. She is adamantly against the proposal, however. She will also present at the same community meeting and wants professional advice as to how to get her points across.

Type of Audience	Goal for the Presentation	Strategy

Case Three

A speaker has come asking for advice. He feels very strongly that special accommodation should be made for Muslim students at the college. His position is that they should not be required to write any scheduled in-class assignments or tests in late afternoon classes during the month of Ramadan so that they can break their fast when the sun sets. He is going to speak at an open student forum.

Type of Audience	Goal for the Presentation	Strategy

Case Four

An employee representative is planning to make a presentation to the board of his company. The employees want the board to consider implementing a flexible workweek, which allows employees to opt for ten-hour days but get three-day weekends.

Type of Audience	Goal for the Presentation	Strategy

Subject

Your research into the subject needs to be thorough. First, keep careful records of all your sources. Your sources might be challenged in a persuasive presentation, so you need to be able to make a case for their reliability. Avoid just taking material from the Internet without validating that the source is credible. Have the names and dates of the sources with you when you present so that you can refer to them if necessary. Have backup examples ready. Second, your research needs to yield precise and specific data. Anticipate as many questions as possible and find out the answers. You can build those questions and answers into your presentation. Finally, be sure that you have a variety of sources. Information that comes primarily from one source is suspect. The more you can show that different sources corroborate what you have to say, the more convincing your case will be.

Benefits

Ask yourself the basic question that the audience will ask. Why should the listener pay attention? More precisely, why should the listener believe what you have to say? In some cases the benefits are immediate and personal, but in others the benefits come over the long term and are not for the listener directly. Consequently, when you make a proposal in your workplace, you will likely stress efficiency or profit or some other aspect that will make the company healthier. On the other hand, you may ask a listener to commit more fully to recycling, not for any immediate or personal benefit, but because that behaviour is consistent with the listener's values for a greater good. Some situations allow you to do both. You can sell the benefits of a gas-efficient car, for example, by emphasizing both the immediate and personal benefits of lower gas costs and the greater good of conservation and environmentalism. Spell these benefits out for yourself before you organize your presentation and highlight them in your talk.

TASK TWO   **Emphasizing the Benefits**

Outline the benefits that the presenters in each of the three cases presented earlier in this unit can emphasize when speaking to the groups.

Case One

IN FAVOUR OF THE HALFWAY HOUSE

Personal Benefits	Other Benefits

Case Two

AGAINST THE HALFWAY HOUSE

Personal Benefits	Other Benefits

Case Three

ACCOMMODATION OF STUDENT NEEDS

Personal Benefits	Other Benefits

Case Four

FLEXIBLE WORK WEEK

Personal Benefits	Other Benefits

Building a Strong Case

A strong case for your presentation is built upon the foundation of solid, verifiable research. But a strong case doesn't end there. The results of research do not speak for themselves. You need to organize those results into a convincing argument that takes the listener step-by-step, premise-by-premise to an irresistible conclusion. That means you need to employ critical thinking, logic, and sound reasoning.

Two traditional approaches are inductive and deductive reasoning. They work like this.

Inductive Reasoning

- Canada eliminated capital punishment and there was no change in the murder rate.
- Germany eliminated capital punishment and there was no change in the murder rate.
- Japan eliminated capital punishment and there was no change in the murder rate.
- Sweden eliminated capital punishment and there was no change in the murder rate.

Conclusion: The evidence is clear that eliminating capital punishment does not mean an escalation in the murder rate. Thus, capital punishment is not a deterrent and should not be reinstated.

If you use this approach, you need to come up with several verifiable cases from which you can draw a conclusion. That conclusion is, in essence, a generalization. Be careful, however, that your generalization is not arrived at too hastily. There may have been other factors working in those countries that account for the results. If there are examples of countries in which the murder did, in fact, climb after the death penalty was eliminated, then you need to account for that—or possibly admit that your line of reasoning is flawed.

Deductive Reasoning

- We should never stand in the way of whatever advances scientific progress.
- Stem cell research advances scientific progress.

Conclusion: We should not stand in the way of stem cell research.

If you use this approach, your argument depends on two items, a major and a minor premise. The major premise is the guiding principle. The minor premise brings in the specific case. If you get the audience to accept these two items, then the conclusion is inescapable. Be careful, however, that you are working with a major premise that your audience can accept. In this case, although certain audiences may indeed find it easy to swallow that scientific progress is the ultimate good, other audiences may not value that. That kind of audience may well accept the minor premise, but because they disagree with the major premise, they never accept your conclusion. Finally, be sure that you have fully identified all three parts of the argument. For example, consider this argument.

- If we raise taxes we will have more money to support the military.

Conclusion: We should raise taxes.

This argument depends on an unspoken major premise. That premise is that we should or need to support the military more. That may well be true, but it is left unexamined in this argument. The presenter needs to state the unspoken major premise and show it to be true before going on with his or her case.

Fallacies

No matter which form of argument you use, examine your argument carefully to be sure that it holds together. You can be sure that your audience, particularly if it disagrees with you from the outset, will find any weaknesses that you allow to slip through. In that case, not only will your presentation fail to convince, it could also be embarrassing. These weaknesses are called fallacies.

Identifying Fallacies TASK THREE

Look at the following passages from the different presentations for the cases earlier in this unit. Each one of the passages demonstrates a reasoning problem. Identify the fallacy and explain to the presenter what the problem is.

Examine the types of fallacies below to choose from, or come up with your own name.

Fallacies
- Red herring: The point is completely unrelated.
- Circular reasoning: The point turns back on itself without support.
- Improper appeal to authority: The point uses testimony from an unqualified person.
- False dichotomy: The point limits the choices to two extremes.
- Hasty generalization: The point makes an unwarranted generalization.
- Band wagon: The point is that the idea is valid because many people hold it.
- Straw man: The point exaggerates a point of the opposition so as to easily refute it.
- Attack on the person: The point takes the attention away from the argument to discredit the source.

Statement	Name of the Problem	Why It's a Problem
The TransCan company instituted the flexible workweek last year. Its business went up 25%.		
The two main people spearheading the campaign for the halfway house in our neighbourhood are not credible. They are ex-convicts themselves.		
If you want to show yourselves as good people, you will support the full accommodation of our needs during our holy season because that is what good people would do.		
You must either support the opening of this halfway house and show yourself to be compassionate or declare yourself against it and expose your intolerance.		

Statement	Name of the Problem	Why It's a Problem
Ex-cons are dangerous people who will more than likely offend again. We can't accept that in our neighbourhood.		
Several popular Canadian artists have spoken out on this issue. They have stood with those who need a halfway house in the community.		
If we allow this halfway house in our neighbourhood, what is next? Are we going to allow drug rehabilitation centres, shelters for sex offenders, and God knows what else? Are we going to allow our beautiful neighbourhood to deteriorate into a slum?		

Considering Objections

A powerful technique in presenting an argument is to deal with objections to your position head on. If you speak to a group about your reasons for holding your position, you really are only speaking about what interests you. If you don't consider what good reasons the listener might have to disagree with you, then you aren't meeting the needs of your audience. A speaker might put together a solid argument that advocates for stronger regulations prohibiting violence and sex on television. The argument might work well from his point of view, but all the time he is speaking the listener is thinking, "That's true, but you're really advocating censorship and censorship is a bad thing." If the speaker never engages the listener's concern about censorship as an attack on the values of a free society, then he will not have much chance of success. He may get the listener to understand his position, but not to agree with it. If you are arguing a controversial point, you can deliver a much stronger presentation if

- you acknowledge the strongest argument against you,
- show that you understand it, and
- show why it isn't valid.

This method is called the thesis–antithesis pattern. First, state your position and make your case with strong, clear support. Then, state the strongest point against you. What is the main argument of those who oppose your position? Next, show what is wrong with that position. Finally, recap and conclude. Here's what it might look like using the case we've just described.

Section	Main Message	Elaboration/Support
Introduction **Thesis**	We need stronger regulations to prohibit sex and violence from broadcasts over public airways.	

Arguments	Effect on children
	             Effect of violent scenes
	
	             Effect of sex scenes
	
	Effect on society in general
	             Effect of violent scenes
	
	             Effect of sex scenes
		Refer to American studies
		
		Refer to Canadian studies
		
		Refer to Canadian studies
		
		Refer to American Studies

Antithesis	Many people are concerned about censorship. They would not support greater regulation of television because they are legitimately concerned about our freedoms.	Censorship is an assault on a democratic society. Freedom of expression is an important right that needs to be protected and nourished.
Refutation	Agree that freedom of expression is precious. At the same time, freedom of expression is also not absolute.	• e.g., we do not have the freedom to slander or libel someone • e.g., we do not have the freedom to print or disseminate hate literature
Conclusion	It is not an either/or situation—completely unregulated public airways or anti-democratic censorship. We have precedents that freedom of expression works within a framework for a healthy society. People can make their own private choices. The seriousness of the effects of violence or sex on public airways, however, calls for the same kind of regulation we put on other harmful expression.	

Thesis–Antithesis Outline   TASK FOUR

As a group, select one of the four clients who came to you in Task One. Work out a thesis–antithesis outline for that client based on the one above. Consider the strongest objection against the speaker's position and advise the speaker how to answer. You can use the form provided.

Section	Main Message	Elaboration/Support
Introduction Thesis		
Arguments		
Antithesis		
Refutation		
Conclusion		

Part One

Person 1: Read the following instructions to the group.

Select an issue on which people disagree and on which you have a strong opinion. That issue could be international, national, local, or something particular to any organization that you are in. Assess where the majority of your audience is likely to stand on the issue, and determine your persuasive goal. Conduct the necessary research, prepare an outline for an 8- to 10-minute presentation, and develop visuals. Be prepared to give your presentation when called upon.

Part Two

Give your presentation. In addition, critique the presentations of your group members using the form provided on page 162 (copy the blank form so you have one form for each presenter). Give the critiques to them as they complete their presentations.

Step Up and Present

Part Three

Read the assessments you received from your group members. Look over your outline and evaluate your presentation. Did it accomplish what you wanted it to? Was there anything you should have done differently? Imagine that you were asked to give the same presentation again. Would you make any changes? Write a brief self-assessment using the spaces provided.

TOPIC:

_____

_____

_____

WHAT I WOULD KEEP IF I DID THE PRESENTATION AGAIN:

_____

_____

_____

WHAT I WOULD DO DIFFERENTLY IF I DID THE PRESENTATION AGAIN:

_____

_____

_____

PRESENTATION CRITIQUE FORM

Assessor's Name_____ For Presenter_____ Topic _____

Oral Delivery   **For Example**

    Volume   Just the right volume ❏

                  Needs more volume ❏

                  Needs less volume ❏

                  Generally appropriate except for ❏

    Voice Colour   Good variety of pitch and rate ❏

                  Needs a greater variety of pitch ❏

                  Needs more variety in rate ❏

                  Generally appropriate except for

Physical Delivery

    Gesture and   Just the right use of natural gesture ❏

    Movement   Needs more gesture ❏

                  Strong, consistent eye contact ❏

                  Needs more eye contact with entire group ❏

                  Excessive movement was distracting ❏

                  Generally appropriate except for

Introduction

    Hook   Effective ❏

                  Needs to be stronger ❏

    Background   Sufficient ❏

                  Needs more background ❏

    Thesis   Clear ❏

                  Needs a clearer thesis statement ❏

Body

    Points   Appropriate number ❏ Needs more ❏ Needs fewer ❏

                  Clear and well supported ❏ Needs more support ❏

                  Well organized ❏ Needs reorganization ❏

                  Clear presentation of antithesis and reasons ❏

                  Antithesis needs to be more firmly presented ❏

                  Clear refutation of antithesis ❏

                  Antithesis needs to be more forcefully refuted ❏

                  Some reasoning flaws ❏ Reduce the number of points ❏

                  Add more points ❏ Clear/well supported ❏

                  Provide more explanation ❏

    Visuals   Effective ❏ Needs ❏

                  Reduce the number of visuals ❏ Add more visuals ❏

                  Visuals need to be clearer ❏

Conclusion   Effective ❏ Included new points ❏ Abrupt ❏

Before the presentation I was

Strongly against ❏ Against ❏ Unaware ❏ Aware, but unconcerned ❏ Agreeable ❏ Strongly agree ❏

After the presentation I was

Strongly against ❏ Against ❏ Unaware ❏ Aware, but unconcerned ❏ Agreeable ❏ Strongly agree ❏

**Additional Comments
and Suggestions:**

OVERALL, I WOULD SAY THAT MY PRESENTATION

_____

_____

_____

Preparing and Delivering a Marketing Presentation   TASK SIX

Part One

Person 2: Read the following instructions to the group.

Select a product or a service to sell to students. You can choose anything at all that requires students to pay. Research the product or service and analyze the students in your group to determine what they think of the product or service you are selling. Determine the benefits, the main selling points, and your strategy. Develop an outline for an 8- to 10-minute sales pitch and prepare any necessary visuals.

Hints

- Be sure to promise only what the product or service can deliver.
- Describe clear benefits to the students.
- Give specific, verifiable information.
- Demonstrate, if possible, or produce testimonials.
- Develop buyer confidence by describing return policies, trial samples, bonuses, introductory offers.
- Use an emotional appeal that stimulates excitement or curiosity.

Part Two

Give your presentation. In addition, critique the presentations of your group members using the form on page 164 (copy the blank form so you have one form for each presenter). Give the critiques to them as they complete their presentations.

Step Up and Present

Part Three

Read the assessments you received from your group members. Look over your outline and evaluate your presentation. Did it accomplish what you wanted it to? Was there anything you should have done differently? Imagine that you were asked to give the same presentation again. Would you make any changes? Write a brief self-assessment using the spaces provided on page 165.

PRESENTATION CRITIQUE FORM

Assessor's Name_____ For Presenter_____ Topic _____

Oral Delivery   **For Example**

Volume   Just the right volume   ❑

Needs more volume   ❑

Needs less volume   ❑

Generally appropriate except for

Voice Colour   Good variety of pitch and rate   ❑

Needs a greater variety of pitch ❑

Needs more variety in rate   ❑

Generally appropriate except for ❑

Physical Delivery

Gesture and   Just the right use of natural gesture   ❑

Movement   Needs more gesture   ❑

Strong, consistent eye contact   ❑

Needs more eye contact with entire group   ❑

Excessive movement was distracting   ❑

Generally appropriate except for ❑

Introduction

Hook   Effective   ❑

Needs to be stronger   ❑

Background   Sufficient   ❑

Needs more background   ❑

Thesis   Clear   ❑

Needs a clearer thesis statement ❑

Body

Points   Appropriate number ❑ Needs more ❑ Needs fewer ❑

Clear and well supported ❑ Needs more support ❑

Well organized ❑ Needs reorganization ❑

Clear presentation of benefits ❑ Benefits need to be more convincing ❑

Confidence well established ❑ Needs to encourage more confidence

outlining return policies, guarantees, or sample offers ❑

Visuals   Effective ❑ Needs ❑

Reduce the number of visuals ❑ Add more visuals ❑

Visuals need to be clearer ❑

Conclusion   Effective ❑ Included new points ❑ Abrupt ❑

**Additional
Comments and
Suggestions:**

TOPIC:

_____

_____

_____

WHAT I WOULD KEEP IF I DID THE PRESENTATION AGAIN:

_____

_____

_____

WHAT I WOULD DO DIFFERENTLY IF I DID THE PRESENTATION AGAIN:

_____

_____

_____

OVERALL, I WOULD SAY THAT MY PRESENTATION

_____

_____

_____

Employment Interviews

You may not think of an employment interview as a presentation at first. At least, it is not like the presentations that you have been giving so far. But when you look at it closely, you begin to see that it has all the elements of a presentation.

1. You need to research both your audience and your subject. Never go into an interview without having found out everything you can about the history of the company, what it does, what its structure is, and what its plans are. You also need to thoroughly research yourself so that you can clearly identify your skills, talents, and experience. Many people leave out so much, whether it be another language that they speak, or skills developed in an unpaid position.

2. Like the marketing presentation, you need to develop a clear list of benefits that the employer will enjoy when you are hired. Knowing those benefits can help you develop your thesis statement about yourself.

3. You need to pay careful attention to your introduction. Just as in a presentation, your interview has an introductory section. The first time you meet the interviewer, that first handshake, the answers to what seem like small-talk questions, "How are you?" or "Did you

have any trouble finding the place?" all set the tone as to the kind of person you are. The first impression or contact determines whether or not the interviewer really wants to get to know you better. Answers to basic questions about your resume provide the background. At some point, find an opportunity to express your thesis statement: that is, the reason you should be hired.

4. Your interview has a body. After you have moved past the preliminaries you will answer various questions. If you are clear as to what your purpose is, the body of your interview will be a series of tightly linked and well-supported points. Your resume has already demonstrated you have the essential qualifications to do the job. Now, you are demonstrating that you are the right personality for this job and this organization. To do that, you need to have a series of stories ready at your fingertips. If you have about 10 stories ready, you will be able to fit them to most of the questions that come up. Like evidence in a persuasive talk, the stories need to be verifiable with places, names, and dates. They need to be convincing examples of your abilities.

5. Prepare a conclusion to your job interview. Be ready to ask specific questions about the company and how you fit in. Those questions should show that you have done some research and are really interested in this particular company as opposed to some other. Move the conclusion to the actual moment of hiring by asking when the decision will be made and arranging for how you will find out about that decision.

6. As you would do with any presentation, practise ahead of time to make your delivery smooth and to develop confidence.

7. Prepare visuals. You could bring a briefcase in where you have extra copies of your resume, copies of your list of references, examples of your work or achievements in a portfolio, a notebook for you to jot down important points and in which you have recorded prepared questions, and whatever else would help you make your case.

TASK SEVEN   Employment Interview

Part One
Each person takes the following questions away and develops a one-paragraph story that answers each.

1. Describe a specific situation in which you encountered and handled conflict.
2. Tell a story that indicates that you work well in a team.
3. Describe an achievement of which you are particularly proud.
4. Identify your best quality. Describe a situation in which that quality was evident.
5. Identify your worst quality. Describe a situation in which that quality was evident.
6. Tell me a story. (Hint: When you get any surprise question like this one, use it to your advantage. Make every question an opportunity to talk about your skills, abilities, and qualities.)
7. What kind of student were you?
8. Describe a situation in which you had to teach or train someone.
9. Tell a story that shows me what kind of problem solver you are.
10. What are your goals? What is the plan for your life?

Part Two

Stand before the other members of the group or the entire class. Answer whatever questions come to you. Remember to keep focused on making every question an opportunity to demonstrate your personality and capabilities.

When you are asking questions, you can choose from the questions in Part One or develop variations on your own. Fill in a critique form for each of the job applicants (make as many copies of the form on page 168 as you need). Give one to each person at the end of the interview.

Part Three

Read the assessments you received from your group members. Look over your outline and evaluate your presentation. Did it accomplish what you wanted it to? Was there anything you should have done differently? Imagine that you are asked to give the same presentation again. Would you make any changes? Write a brief self-assessment using the spaces below.

TOPIC:

WHAT I WOULD KEEP IF I DID THE PRESENTATION AGAIN:

WHAT I WOULD DO DIFFERENTLY IF I DID THE PRESENTATION AGAIN:

OVERALL, I WOULD SAY THAT MY PRESENTATION

PRESENTATION CRITIQUE FORM

Assessor's Name _____ For Presenter _____ Topic _____

			For Example
Oral Delivery			
Volume	Just the right volume	❑	
	Needs more volume	❑	
	Needs less volume	❑	
	Generally appropriate except for	❑	
Voice Colour	Good variety of pitch and rate	❑	
	Needs a greater variety of pitch	❑	
	Needs more variety in rate	❑	
	Generally appropriate except for	❑	
Physical Delivery			
Gesture and	Just the right use of natural gesture	❑	
Movement	Needs more gesture	❑	
	Strong, consistent eye contact	❑	
	Needs more eye contact	❑	
	Excessive movement was distracting	❑	
	Generally appropriate except for	❑	
Confidence			
	Effective and self-assured	❑	
	Needs to be more confident	❑	
	Sufficient	❑	
Response to Questions			
	Appropriate length	❑	
	Needs to be longer	❑	
	Needs to be shorter	❑	
	Clear and well supported	❑	
	Needs more support	❑	
	Well organized	❑	
	Needs re-organization	❑	
	Clear presentation of benefits	❑	
	Benefits need to be more convincing	❑	
	Generally effective	❑	
	Effective, except for	❑	
Additional Comments and Suggestions:			

In Summary

Take three minutes to write a summary of what you learned from participating in the tasks of Unit 13.

_____

_____

_____

_____

_____

_____

_____

_____

_____

_____

_____

_____

_____

_____

_____

_____

_____

_____

_____

_____

_____

_____

UNIT 14

Group Presentations

Here's what you'll work on in this unit.

- Preparing and delivering a group presentation
- Mapping an issue
- Determining effective strategies for collaborative research and delivery
- Determining strategies for answering questions
- Critiquing, reviewing, and revising a group presentation

You have been asked to give several presentations in this book. Although you worked with your group giving and getting feedback on preparation, outlines, and delivery, you have given the presentations on your own. You will encounter occasions, however, that ask you to present with others. An employer might put you on a team to research a topic, devise a policy, or come up with a proposal for a client. You may find yourself working on a very complex subject that would be difficult for one person to prepare in the available time. Working on a group presentation, however, allows you to focus on those areas in which you have a particular interest.

This unit will ask that your group work together in a different way from previous chapters. You will work together on a group project that requires everyone to pull together for a single purpose and present the results of that work in a single presentation.

TASK ONE   Preparing and Delivering a Group Presentation

The group will investigate a problem or issue in the college. Your goal is to clearly present the problem, determine its causes and background, present hard data, and propose a solution. You have a 25- to 30-minute time slot. Your audience is whoever in the college has the power to make the changes you want.

Part One

Select a group facilitator, timekeeper, and recorder for the work in this task. The group can decide, if it wishes, to rotate the responsibilities.

Setting the stage for the upcoming work, rather than plunging right in, is an important step to a successful group presentation. Your instructor will tell you how many planning sessions you have to accomplish this project. This unit will break the task down for you, but you need to decide what has to be in place to get the work done. Meet as a group and establish some ground rules for operating. What is essential for getting the task done that should be spelled out at the beginning? Should everyone agree to an attendance policy? How will the work sessions be run? What can the group agree upon now to do when a difference of opinion comes up later? How will you resolve it and proceed?

GROUND RULES FOR THE GROUP PRESENTATION PROJECT

Part Two (20 minutes)

Identify as many issues in the college as possible. Record them in the form provided. Avoid any discussion around the issues at this point. Your purpose is to record as many alternative topics as possible.

ISSUES AND/OR PROBLEMS

Part Three (10 minutes)

Discuss the proposed topics. Which one has the best potential for your group presentation? Which one is in the top three choices of everyone? Which one seems both interesting and doable? Consider the kind of research that would be necessary and the feasibility of getting that research accomplished in your time frame.

SELECTED ISSUE/PROBLEM

Part Four (15 minutes)

Break down your issue into its component parts.

- What is the current situation?
- Who is involved?
- What is the history behind the situation?
- Just why is this issue important to your college community?
- What is the best solution?
- What does that solution require?

Each of these answers will likely also suggest subdivisions. One way to accomplish this task is to produce a map that uses large circles branching to small ones. Here is an example.

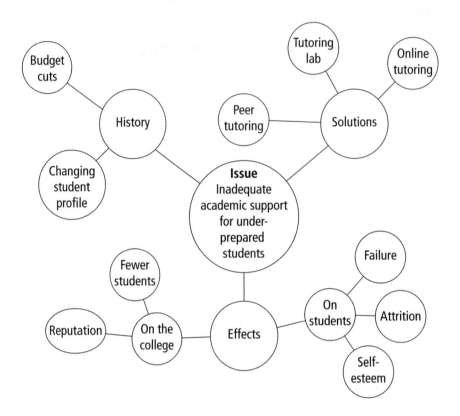

Figure 14.1

When you map out the issue in this way, your group can better see the component parts of the problem. Don't limit yourself as you create your own map. Follow the branches as far as your thinking takes you. You won't research everything or present every branch, but the more branches you make, the greater the selection you have as to what will go in the final presentation. Call out whatever branches or new units of the problem occur to you so that your recorder can produce the group map. You can use the box provided.

Part Five (20 minutes)

At this point the group can break up the work so that you have specialists in the different parts of the problem. The job of the specialist is to become an expert in one of the areas of your group map. In the example above, someone might become a specialist in the history of the issue, while someone else specializes in the effect. You may also choose to have more than one specialist for an area. The group presenting on Inadequate Academic Support might, for example, have one Effects specialist for the effects on the student, while having another Effects specialist for the effects on the college. It is important that these specialists work for the group rather than just for themselves. That is, the specialists need to report what they have learned at different stages of the project. In that way, the whole group has access to the information that the members might want to refer to in their own parts of the presentation.

The group can also help each specialist by suggesting research sources. The group working on Inadequate Academic Support could come up with something like the following.

Specialty	Research Sources
History: Budget cuts	• Interview financial officers in the college • Interview staff who were at the college before and after the budget cuts • Consult back copies of the college news
History: Changing student profile	• Interview staff in admissions as to how the student profile is changing • Interview staff in the special needs office • Interview various professors regarding academic challenges to the students • Conduct a survey using a questionnaire in the cafeteria to get student opinion on the problem
Effects on students	• Interview college counselling staff • Consult the guidance department report • Include questions on the survey regarding the impact on students
Effects on the college	• Consult the college's reports on attrition and student satisfaction • Conduct a survey in your community using a questionnaire regarding the college's reputation
Solutions: Peer tutoring	• Contact other colleges where it is offered and determine what resources were needed to institute the program and what impact it has had • Use the Internet and electronic databases to search for any studies on the effectiveness of peer tutoring.
Solutions: Tutoring centre	• Contact other colleges where it is offered and determine what resources were needed to institute the program and what impact it has had • Use the Internet and electronic databases to search for any studies on the effectiveness of tutoring centres
Solutions: Online tutoring	• Contact other colleges where it is offered and determine what resources were needed to institute the program and what impact it has had • Use the Internet and electronic databases to search for any studies on the effectiveness of online tutoring

This table is only one way of looking at the issue. The group may also decide that it wants a separate unit on the benefits of providing better academic support or a unit on the resources necessary to carry out its proposals. The presentation could go in many directions. It depends on how the group has analyzed the listeners.

One of the things that this table shows is that you can piggyback on the research of other specialists. For example, if the group decides that a survey of the student population would provide useful data for the presentation, it may be that the results of some questions could be used by more than one unit. Another possibility is that the group might want to add additional questions so that the one survey provides direct information for more than one specialist. In that case, different specialists from different areas could work together in composing, administering, and analyzing the survey.

Use the following table to determine the units, specialists, and type of research.

Specialty	Type of Research	Name of Specialist

Part Six (one hour)

As you collect your information and share it with the other members of the group, you can begin to work out the shape of the group presentation. An important concept to keep in mind is that the presentation is, indeed, a group presentation. It should not seem like a string of individual presentations that have been prepared in isolation. You can create a cohesive, organic, and effective structure by using a few techniques in your planning.

Select a facilitator. The facilitator will be the glue that holds the presentation together by providing context for the presentation. That person will open and close the presentation as well as help the presentation move effortlessly from part to part by providing bridging information or introductions of the other speakers.

Present together. Work together rather than alone in a group presentation. If one area of your topic has more than one specialist, then they can present together. If not, your presentation still can make use of group support. You might invite another group member to hold up a visual for you, operate the PowerPoint program at the moment you need it, or help you with a demonstration.

Link the presentation units. Refer to specific points made in other parts of the group presentation. In that way, you cement the units. They are no longer separate units, but rather they integrate into a greater structure.

Use transitions. Unlike your expository and persuasive presentations, you will not each have an introduction and conclusion. The facilitator will provide an introduction and conclusion to the group presentation. On the other hand, your own part of the group presentation still needs an opening and a closing. In this case, however, the opening is a transition from an earlier unit, and your closing is a transition to the next unit. The transition should be a short bridge that shows the listener clearly what the new unit is and why the listener is being taken there.

Use the following form to plan out the order of your presentation, the visuals you will use, and who will be involved in each unit. Use the various techniques you employed in your expository outline. Since your presentation has a persuasive element, consider whether or not the group presentation needs an antithesis and refutation.

Unit	Content	Visuals	Group Members

Part Seven (one to two hours)

Once your research is in and you have devised a method of presentation, it is time to rehearse. You have several goals here. The group needs to determine

1. whether or not the entire presentation fits in the assigned time frame,
2. what adjustments need to be made to individual presentations,
3. if the visuals work well,
4. if there are any gaps in the presentation which require information or explanation.

1. Whether or not the entire presentation fits in the assigned time frame

You have 25 to 30 minutes. Does the presentation run over? If so, what can you cut? What is it that takes time that could be shortened or even sacrificed? If you are under time then you need to decide where you can amplify. Where could you present more hard data? Are there any implications which have not been fully discussed?

2. What adjustments need to be made to individual presentations

Group members can give critiques to each presenter in the same way that they did for expository and persuasive presentations. You will find the forms for this critique on pages 181 and 182. Fill out the critiques, but use them for a roundtable discussion of each segment after it is presented. The goal in this case is to come to a consensus as to what changes would be best for the presentation as a whole.

Hint

You will need one critique form for each presenter. Reproduce the form on page 181 so you have as many as needed. Check off the appropriate boxes and indicate specific examples of what you mean by your comment in the For Example column. Write specific suggestions and comments at the bottom. Guest listeners can also use the same form. If you give the form to people outside the group, explain how to fill it out and in particular how to give concrete and constructive criticism.

---

3. If the visuals work well

It is not necessary, or even desirable, for each part of the group presentation to use visuals. Too many visuals could easily become tiresome. The visuals need to be appropriate and memorable. As you watch the group presentation unfold, ask yourself if the visuals are used at the right moment, if they really help carry the point, and if they are likely to make a strong impression.

4. If there are any gaps in the presentation that require information or explanation

It can be very difficult for a group to determine gaps in its own presentation. After all, group members have been working on the project for some time, sharing research and critiquing each other's presentations. Most of you will automatically fill in any gaps without realizing that the listener might not be able to do that. In this case, it is very helpful to have someone you know sit in on the presentation to give feedback. Is there anything that your guest or guests don't quite get? That response can help you fine-tune your work.

Arrange for a question period at the end of the presentation. Here are some guidelines.

- Everyone in the group should be available and visible.
- The facilitator should announce the question period and indicate how much time is available.
- The facilitator should manage the questions. That means selecting the people who want to ask questions, arranging the order of the questions and referring the questions to the right person in the group.
- Listen fully to any question asked of you. If you know the answer, give a concise reply and refer to the sources. If you do not know the answer, say so, and ask if anyone else in the group knows. Hand the question over to that person or to the facilitator.
- Answer any brief follow-up, but avoid getting into a long discussion with one person. You can offer to speak with that person afterwards. The facilitator should also step in to give other people a chance to ask questions.

Step Up and Present

Part Eight (30 minutes)

After you have researched, planned, and rehearsed, present the results to the class.

Fill in the presentation evaluation sheet for each of the other groups that you hear present. Give them to the facilitator when the group is done.

Hint

Use the form on page 182 and make as many copies as you need for your group. Remember that one very important critique is whether or not each presentation fits smoothly with the rest.

PRESENTATION CRITIQUE FORM

Assessor's Name_____ For Presenter_____ Topic_____

Oral Delivery			For Example

Oral Delivery

Volume
- Just the right volume ❑
- Needs more volume ❑
- Needs less volume ❑
- Generally appropriate except for ❑

Voice Colour
- Good variety of pitch and rate ❑
- Needs a greater variety of pitch ❑
- Needs more variety in rate ❑
- Generally appropriate except for ❑

Physical Delivery

Gesture and Movement
- Just the right use of natural gesture ❑
- Needs more gesture ❑
- Strong, consistent eye contact ❑
- Needs more eye contact with entire group ❑
- Excessive movement was distracting ❑
- Generally appropriate except for ❑

Introduction

Hook
- Effective ❑
- Needs to be stronger ❑

Background
- Sufficient ❑
- Needs more background ❑

Thesis
- Clear ❑
- Needs a clearer thesis statement ❑

Body

Points
- Appropriate number ❑
- Reduce the number of points ❑
- Add more points ❑
- Clear/well supported ❑
- Provide more explanation ❑

Visuals
- Effective ❑
- Reduce the number of visuals ❑
- Add more visuals ❑
- Visuals need to be clearer ❑

Conclusion
- Effective ❑
- Included new points ❑
- Abrupt ❑
- Needs ❑

Additional Comments and Suggestions:

PRESENTATION EVALUATION SHEET

Your Name_____   For Group Presentation _____

The presentation was

❏   informative

❏   generally informative except for _____

❏   needs to be more informative

❏   convincing

❏   generally convincing except for _____

❏   needs to be more convincing

❏   smooth and cohesive with effective transitions

❏   generally cohesive except for _____

❏   needs to be less a series of individual presentations and more a group presentation

The most effective part of the presentation was

The least effective part of the presentation was

Additional Comments and Suggestions:

Part Nine (10 minutes)

Look over your contribution to the group project and evaluate your presentation. Did it accomplish what you wanted it to? Was there anything you should have done differently? Imagine that you were asked to give the same presentation again. Would you make any changes? Write a brief self-assessment using the spaces provided.

TOPIC:

_____

_____

_____

WHAT I WOULD KEEP IF I DID THE PRESENTATION AGAIN:

_____

_____

_____

WHAT I WOULD DO DIFFERENTLY IF I DID THE PRESENTATION AGAIN:

_____

_____

_____

OVERALL, I WOULD SAY THAT MY PRESENTATION

_____

_____

Part Ten (30 minutes)

Consider the group presentation. Did it accomplish what it was supposed to? Was there anything that the group should have done differently? Imagine that the group was asked to give the same presentation again. Would you recommend any changes? Write a brief self-assessment using the space on page 184. Bring the page to a group meeting to discuss the presentation. Use the follow-up forms of your group and the critique forms from the class to evaluate whether or not the group was successful.

TOPIC:

_____

_____

_____

WHAT DID THE GROUP DO WELL THAT SHOULD BE KEPT?

_____

_____

_____

WHAT SHOULD THE GROUP DO DIFFERENTLY?

_____

_____

_____

OVERALL, I WOULD SAY THAT THE GROUP PRESENTATION

_____

_____

_____

In Summary

Take three minutes to write a summary of what you learned from participating in the tasks of Unit 14.

_____

_____

_____

_____

_____

_____

_____

_____

_____

UNIT 15

Speaking at Meetings

Here's what you'll work on in this unit.

- Preparing and delivering three different types of impromptu presentations as part of a discussion at a meeting
- Identifying essential techniques for leading an effective meeting
- Developing additional techniques for ensuring a successful meeting

The expository, persuasive, and group presentations that you have been asked to give all allowed for research, planning, and rehearsal. You will also find yourself in situations when you have to speak spontaneously or impromptu. One of these situations is the meeting. Your employer may ask you to participate in regular meetings or call you into a meeting especially called for a specific issue. Although you may know the agenda of these meetings ahead of time and so know the general topics to be considered, you won't really know the direction the meeting will take. You might suddenly hear a proposal that you just know would be the wrong thing to do. In the course of listening to other people you might suddenly have an idea that would be helpful. In those situations, you need to present. This presentation, though, is totally different from the presentations you have given earlier because now you have only the sketchiest notion of what your own presentation will be like. It will actually take shape as you give it. This kind of presentation, however, can be very important. If you present your viewpoint well, the entire meeting can shift gears. If you do not present well, the vote taken at the end of the meeting might just go the way you wish it wouldn't. If you don't present at all because you are not sure how to state your case, then your viewpoint never even gets heard.

If you're presenting at the meeting as part of the agenda, then you will likely give a full presentation that fits in an assigned length. You will use the various devices and techniques discussed in this book. If you are not presenting as part of the agenda, but are making an impromptu presentation as part of the general discussion, then you need to give a convincing presentation that states your points powerfully and succinctly. You can use one of the formulas in this unit of the book until you become comfortable enough to present from instinct.

Expressing a Point of View

One way to present your point of view is to use a method that is easy to memorize. Each of the methods below has been reduced to an acronym to make it easy to remember.

OMER

This system is the basic approach to expressing an opinion at a meeting.

Opinion: State your opinion on the subject in one brief sentence. That sentence should include the focus, subject, and specific point of view.

Instituting	a flexible workweek	makes a lot of sense.
Focus	**Subject**	**Point of View**

Main Reason: Present one clear reason for holding your point of view in one sentence.

> Staff that no longer has to worry about issues outside the workplace would be less distracted on the job.

Example: Present one clear example that makes your reason concrete in one sentence.

> For example, some parents on staff here would be glad to start work earlier if that meant they could get home in time so that their children would not be alone after school.

Restate the opinion: End your presentation with a short sentence that recasts your first sentence in different words.

> So, it would be a good idea for our company to start an adjustable work-time policy.

SOME ARE

This system is a fuller version of the one above.

Start: Begin with a one-sentence introduction that identifies an issue.

> Many senior staff members have expressed the need over the last few years for a better arrangement of office hours.

Opinion: State your opinion on the subject in one brief sentence. That sentence should include the focus, subject, and specific point of view.

Instituting	a flexible workweek	makes a lot of sense.
Focus	**Subject**	**Point of View**

Main Reason: Present one clear reason for holding your point of view in one sentence.

> Staff that no longer has to worry about issues outside the workplace would be less distracted on the job.

Example: Present one clear example that makes your reason concrete in one sentence.

> For example, some parents on staff here would be glad to start work earlier if that meant they could get home in time so that their children would not be alone after school.

Advantage: Add one sentence that clearly demonstrates the benefit to the company.

> A company in Vancouver that made this change found that staff became 10 percent more productive.

Restate the opinion: End your presentation with a short sentence that recasts your first sentence in different words.

> So, it would be a good idea for our company to start an adjustable work-time policy.

SOME AFAR

This system incorporates the antithesis or the opposing viewpoint in your argument. This method is the strongest of the three presented here.

Start: Begin with a one-sentence introduction that identifies an issue.

> Many senior staff members have expressed the need over the last few years for a better arrangement of office hours.

Opinion: State your opinion on the subject in one brief sentence. That sentence should include the focus, subject, and the specific point of view.

Instituting	a flexible workweek	makes a lot of sense.
Focus	**Subject**	**Point of View**

Main Reason: Present one clear reason for holding your point of view in one sentence.

> Staff that no longer has to worry about issues outside the workplace would be less distracted on the job.

Example: Present one clear example that makes your reason concrete in one sentence.

> For example, some parents on staff here would be glad to start work earlier if that meant they could get home in time so that their children would not be alone after school.

Antithesis: Clearly state the main objection already raised or likely to be raised to the idea.

> One of the problems with a flexible work week is trying to schedule meetings when not everyone is at the office.

Refute: Show why the objection is either incorrect or how the problem can be solved.

> But flextime usually has to do with starting and ending the day. Everyone will be in the office during the bulk of the workday. We could schedule regular meetings then. If we needed a special early meeting on occasion, then all we need to do is notify everyone in advance.

Advantage: Add one sentence that clearly demonstrates the benefit to the company.

> A company in Vancouver that made this change found that staff became 10 percent more productive.

Restate the opinion: End your presentation with a short sentence that recasts your first sentence in different words.

> So, it would be a good idea for our company to start an adjustable work time policy.

Hint

You can use these three formulas to work out a tight, well-planned presentation in just a few minutes. Simply write down the acronym of the method you want to use, whether it be OMER, SOME ARE, or SOME AFAR. Then, jot down what you want to say beside each of the letters. Refer to that sheet of paper as you speak up. Later, you will find you will be able to do it without writing anything down first.

Speaking Up at Meetings	TASK ONE

Step Up and Present

Person 4: Read out the directions and facilitate this activity using the schedule below.

Person 3: Keep time. Each person has one minute for each presentation.

Choose an issue, but not an opinion on that issue, that you will give to one of the people in the group according to the table on page 190. The topic can be connected to your college, field, or governance.

Someone will also give you a topic. Take a few moments to develop a presentation on the topic given to you using one of the methods discussed above.

Give the presentation to the group. When you are finished, ask the group for feedback as to how effective your presentation was and what you could do the next time to improve it. Use the feedback questions below the schedule.

Step	Issues	Process
1.	Person 2: Give a topic to Person 1.	Prepare for one minute and present for one minute.
2.	Person 3: Give a topic to Person 4.	Group: Give feedback to person 1 while person 4 prepares. Person 4: Present after the feedback session.
3.	Person 1: Give a topic to Person 2.	Group: Give feedback to person 4 while person 2 prepares. Person 2: Present after the feedback session.
4.	Person 4: Give a topic to Person 3.	Group: Give feedback to person 2 while person 3 prepares. Person 3: Present after the feedback session.

Feedback Questions

IS THE POINT OF VIEW CLEARLY EXPRESSED?

IS THE POINT OF VIEW WELL SUPPORTED? WHAT COULD MAKE THE SUPPORT STRONGER?

DOES THE PRESENTATION HAVE AN EFFECTIVE CONCLUSION? WHAT COULD MAKE THE CONCLUSION MORE EFFECTIVE?

Leading a Meeting

You have participated in planning meetings with your group to accomplish the tasks in this book. Those meetings were likely informal. Sometimes organizations opt for a formal approach following particular procedures for making motions, taking votes, and running discussions. Whether the meeting is informal or formal, the leader or facilitator can contribute to the success of the meeting in a number of ways.

Devise a Clear Agenda. In some cases, you can write the agenda ahead of time and get it to the participants before they come. Everyone has a chance to think about the issues ahead of time and prepare some comments. One way to make a meeting successful is to keep the agenda simple. Too many items on an agenda means that discussion time for each item needs to be severely curtailed. A rushed agenda means rushed decisions that might give you problems later. It is better to have more meetings with fewer items than fewer meetings with a large number of items.

In other cases, you can determine the agenda at the beginning of the meeting. Ask the participants what items are to be put on the table. Spend the first few minutes getting a consensus on the top few items that should be discussed right away.

Guide the Discussion. Keep the discussion focused by intervening when the discussion has gone off the agreed-upon agenda items. This was your task as facilitator for many of the discussions needed to accomplish your tasks. Tell the group that you will note the topic down for the next meeting, and return to the original topic.

Keep Track of the Time. You were timekeeper for some of the tasks. Your job was to remind the group of how much time was left. Participants in a meeting appreciate clear time frames for meetings. They should know before they come, or at the very latest at the beginning of the meeting, just how long the meeting will take. If you are leading the meeting, stick to the announced time line. Avoid going over by allotting a specific amount of time to each agenda item. Announce just how much time is left for each item. If the group wants the discussion to keep going, give them the choice of either deleting another agenda item and using that time, or continuing the discussion at the next meeting.

Manage the Meeting Equitably. One of your tasks as facilitator was to be sure that everyone had an opportunity to speak. It may be necessary to intervene at some point if someone has used a great deal of time and invite anyone else who has an idea to speak. Sometimes you might want to ask a specific question of someone who has not spoken for a while to encourage some contribution.

Leading Meetings   TASK TWO

Part One
Person 3: Facilitate this task. Make sure everyone has an opportunity to speak.

Person 2: Record the results in the table on page 192.

Person 1: Keep time. The group has 15 minutes to accomplish this task.

Person 4: Be ready to present the findings to the class.

You have participated in group meetings and work sessions throughout this book. Use that experience and your experience in various other kinds of meetings to add on to the list given above on leading and running meetings. What can a leader do to increase the chances of a successful meeting?

RUNNING AN EFFECTIVE MEETING

1.	
2.	
3.	
4.	
5.	
6.	
7.	
8.	
9.	
10.	

Step Up and Present

Part Two

Person 4: Present the findings of your group to the class.

Group members, add any new ideas that you hear to your list.

In Summary

Take three minutes to write a summary of what you learned from participating in the tasks of Unit 15.

_____

_____

_____

_____

_____

_____

_____

_____

_____

_____

_____

_____

_____

_____

_____

_____

_____

_____

_____

_____

Closing Notes

This book on presentation skills began with preparation, continued with delivery, and finished with applications. You reflected on your own work and on the work of your group members in each of these parts. Now that you have completed this book, look back on what you have done. One of your first tasks at the beginning in Unit 1 was to develop a list of personal objectives from which you put together a goal statement. Go back to those objectives and goal statement now. Reflect on whether or not you have achieved them. You can use the following forms to help you organize your thoughts.

Hint

Work on the tasks in the conclusion individually. You can, of course, consult your group members, but it is not necessary for you to do so or to show the work you do in this section to them. Take your time, look at your answers to questions throughout the book, and reread some of your critique forms before coming up with a response.

PERSONAL OBJECTIVES FOR THE BOOK

OBJECTIVES ATTAINED:
OBJECTIVES PARTIALLY ATTAINED:
OBJECTIVES NOT YET ATTAINED:
WHAT NEEDS TO BE DONE:

GOAL STATEMENT

Fully achieved __   Mostly Achieved __   Partially Achieved __   Not Achieved __

ELABORATE ON YOUR ANSWER.

You put together a list of delivery tips for an effective presentation in Unit 6. At that time, you also assessed how skilled you were. Take a look at that list again. In particular, look at the ones that you rated "I really need to work on this one." Based on the critiques from your classmates and instructor, would you give yourself a higher rating for any of these now? Are there any that remain unchanged?

SPECIFIC PRESENTATION SKILLS

IMPROVED SKILLS:

SKILLS STILL REQUIRING IMPROVEMENT:

A useful exercise at the end of a book like this one is to identify what you found easy and what you found more challenging. That will help identify your strengths and weaknesses. If you can clearly name your biggest challenge, the better you will be able to meet and handle it. Which one of the presentations was the easiest to put together and deliver? Which one was the most problematic?

| EASIEST PRESENTATION: |
| THE REASON IT WAS EASY WAS |
| MOST DIFFICULT PRESENTATION: |
| THE REASON IT WAS DIFFICULT WAS |

This book depended on developing a habit of constant self-reflection based upon the critique of your audience, your classmates, and your instructor. It took this approach because your growth as an effective presenter requires you to constantly assess and refine your work. When you are able to accept criticism, reflect honestly on your own work, and learn from the strengths and weaknesses of other presenters, you will find that your skills will sharpen and improve. This process is a continual one. It begins with this book, but continues with every presentation you give as you hone your abilities to become an ever more effective presenter.